MW01174129

Life in the Ruins
(An Urban Missiology
for the 21st Century Church)

Daniel MacKinnon

Cover Photo by John Edmonds
greeneggscreative@mac.com

ISBN: 9798867152567

DEDICATION

This book is dedicated to all the pastors and church leaders who faithfully have served their congregations and ministries through all the shifting sands of time, culture, and the upheaval of COVID, and yet have kept their eyes on Jesus, continuing to man their mission outposts in partnership with the Lord of the Harvest for His glory.

TABLE OF CONTENTS

INTRODUCTION:
(RUINS AND SWAMPS)

As a kid growing up in Cape Breton, we used to spend a lot of time visiting my grandfather in Louisbourg. One of the things we often did was wander around the site of the old French fortress, which at that time was the remnants of a few two-foot stone walls around a field, before the reconstruction took place. One of the amazing things about walking that property some three hundred years after the French and English had exchanged a vigorous cannonball trade was that if you stuck your toe in the ground, you often turfed up pieces of broken pottery and other treasures, evidence of the thriving community that once lived there. I see in those old ruins a picture of the church today, especially in Canada; evidence of once thriving communities of faith that have seen monumental shifts in their worlds.

When the first SHREK movie was released, I was struck by the similarities in the situation of Shrek and the Canadian Church, although, truth to be told, it probably is descriptive of the Church in general of the West. Let me explain.

Shrek is an ogre who lives semi-contentedly in his swamp. It is a semi-contented because it is really the only place he feels safe in a world that continually vilifies ogres and in which he has had many occasions of being wounded by the actions and messages of the non-ogre world. To ensure his safety Shrek has himself posted signs all around his swamp telling people to "Keep Out" and created sufficient experiences of fear to minimize traffic.

Then one day everything changes. Shrek becomes aware of rustlings around his swamp and noises in his cottage that would indicate the presence of others and what he discovers is indeed troubling to him. His swamp has been filled with fairy-tale creatures of all descriptions who have been deposited in his swamp by the king who wants them removed from his life and kingdom. When he tries to rid himself of this unwanted occupation, he learns that the only way he can get his life returned to "normal" is to go on a quest to rescue a princess in a tower. What follows in the movie is the adventure and eventual love story of Shrek as he and his talking Donkey rescue the princess.

It seems to me that Shrek is like the church today. Our world has changed all around us. Where once the church operated out of a Christendom model of power and acceptance that influenced the world in which it existed now instead, in our post-modern, pre-Christian world we find ourselves in lost within our own culture without ever having moved. The world around us is hostile and dismissive of the Christian Gospel as being too narrow and the Church as being too irrelevant, or out of step with the political correctness of the broader culture.

In many respects the messages communicated by the larger culture, which is for the most part pagan and unchurched, would suggest that it would be quite content if we all went away, and in many ways she has. The continuous decline in attendance in our churches tells us that something is wrong. COVID turned up the intensity of the problem as it served as both a dividing and isolating factor in our churches, from which most churches have struggled to recover. A crisis is looming, if not already upon us.

How we have understood ourselves in the past based on assumed respect and power needs to be updated to meet the changing landscape we find ourselves navigating. In our current time, we are not respected, our influence is minimal, usually one life at a time rather than on a whole community, and culture is now influencing the church more than church is influencing culture.

The church can no longer function in the model of Christendom where we were part of the dominant culture, shaping values, and influencing governments. Instead, we find ourselves in a missionary encounter with our culture, a counter-culture movement more like the first century of the church than perhaps any other time in the life of the community of Christ. We find ourselves living among the ruins of another day, in a swamp as it were, where our world has turned upside down, the values we cherished have all but evaporated, and where there are no guarantees of our future existence, evidenced in once "Christian" nations that are now determined secular states or under control of other religions.

I believe it is time to rediscover our "quest" and that is where Jeremiah 29 offers so much insight for how God's people can be missionaries and influence the world around them. This book is an attempt to mine out some of the deep truths found in the urban missionary strategy the prophet Jeremiah gave the exiles who were carried off to Babylon. Their world was turned upside down, not by their choice, but for their benefit and the benefit of those with whom they would be living.

Is it possible the church today is being called to a missionary encounter within its own culture? Is it possible our world has turned upside down for our benefit and benefit of the bigger world we live in, depending on how we respond to the opportunity presented to us? The Chinese characters for crisis when translated into English form a compound word– probably best translated "precarious moment" or "precarious change-point" a moment of change that has some element of danger in it; danger presented either as opportunity for action or danger from inaction.

The response of many in the church today is to adopt a fortress mentality to either bunker down and wait for the coming end of the world, to hang on to each other in a holy huddle and say let the world go to Hell where it is headed and we'll stay pure ourselves, or man the guns on the walls and fire our canons from the sterility of the fortress at every target that doesn't talk like us, act like us, or believe like us.

Others adopt a mentality of accommodation where we surrender our distinctives as followers of Christ and become a religious expression of the broader culture. Cultures' values become our values and the church increasingly becomes the religious golden retriever, only happy if it is pleasing everyone. Then the cross then becomes a shadow, the Saviour becomes an option, the Bible a collection of religious stories open to a multitude of interpretations, and the narrow way becomes a lost path. It seems to me that neither the fortress nor the golden retriever mentalities reflect very healthy options for how to ministry effectively today.

I believe instead that we are living in a "precarious moment" as challenging as the one given the first disciples after the ascension of Christ, to "go and make disciples of all the nations." Our going will begin with an embracing of where we are actually living today, to love the communities we live in, to build small and build lots, to be fruitful for the sake of others and the community; to essentially follow Jeremiah's instructions to the exiles in Jeremiah 29;

"Build houses and settle down; (vs.5a)
Plant gardens and eat what they produce. (vs. 5b)
Marry and have sons and daughters… (vs. 6)
Seek the peace and the prosperity of the city to which I have carried you. (vs. 7a)
Pray for its prosperity. (vs. 7b)
Encourage truth telling. (vs. 8-9)
Trust in God's plans (vs.10-11)
Seek the Lord with all your heart (vs. 12-14)

May God raise up a generation of people willing to embrace God's precarious moment by adopting His missionary strategy for His people, and may we begin to influence our world one changed life at a time.

It's my theory that those exiles, people like Daniel, Hananiah, Azariah, and Mishael may very well have influenced the dominant culture of Babylon to the extent that "wise men" would go seeking the Messiah at the time of the incarnation. Those wise men, having come under the influence of the "minority culture" and their Scripture, led them to follow the Bethlehem star, bearing their prophetic gifts of gold, frankincense and myrrh, and then worshipping Him.

CHAPTER ONE

WHO MOVED?

Jeremiah 29:4
This is what the Lord Almighty, the God of Israel, says to all those I carried into exile from Jerusalem to Babylon:

"We live in a Babylon world. In Babylon, the anti-God city, everything is based on the market. Everything is market. (That's what the mark of the beast is about: when you can't buy or sell without selling out, you have acquiesced in the reign of evil.)"

Leonard Sweet - *I Am A Follower*

When I arrived at seminary, I was told that if I believed the things I did I should be in another denomination. That set up quite a puzzle for me as I didn't believe anything but what had been the historic standards of the church. Pretty clearly something had changed and the question I was left with was "Who moved?" It wasn't me and it wasn't the historic standards like the Westminster Confession of Faith on the essence of the Gospel. Since that time, a lot of things have moved in our world, not just theologically but culturally and morally as well.

I grew up on an island in the east coast of Canada. The people of that island, Cape Breton, are known to have a unique identity/culture, not unlike other island cultures of either the east coast or the world in general. Our culture was steeped in the Celtic teapot but with its own local flavors added. Gaelic was still a living language on the island and the Gaelic College was world renowned. At the time I was growing up on the island it seemed like there were pipers out practicing in the backyards of almost every block in summertime. The people at the time still lived off the sea, the forests, the rich coal mines, and the steel industry as the main sources of employment. Steeped in Celtic culture they had their own micro culture as an island people but in general it was a time marked more by underemployment than anything else, as well as some of the broader contextual issues of the sixties and seventies.

When I moved to the mainland (Halifax), to attend university, it was a move from a city of 30,000 people to a city of 500,000. As you can imagine it meant a shift for me, not the least of which was living in a "foreign" culture. They still spoke the same language and had many similarities but "this was not Kansas!" I found myself living in a similar but different culture.

When I moved from Halifax to Toronto (500,000 people to 1,000,000+ people) I found myself living in another culture again, similar in that they still mostly spoke English, though with a TV non-accent, but very different in many ways. Sydney, where I had grown up hosted a microcosm of the world in those days due to the steel and mining industries, but Toronto had a macrocosm. It seemed like the whole world lived in Toronto. It was so different that in the taxi ride from Pearson Airport to downtown Toronto I thought the plane had taken a wrong turn somewhere because I hardly saw a white person in the other cars along the twenty-minute freeway ride to the University of Toronto campus. This was definitely not Kansas, Dorothy!

Life brings about a lot of changes, not the least of which are the changes that happen around us in our culture. Remember when you had to go to the library or the bookstore to get the research materials you needed to do your homework instead of touching a picture on your iPad? Remember when you used a typewriter for your school papers because your teacher stopped accepting handwritten assignments she couldn't read? And then remember your first computer that covered the top of your desk requiring all kinds of disks to do what we now would consider the simplest tasks, tasks now done simpler and faster by your cell phone. I remember bringing home my first computer, an IBM PCjr, setting it up with great anticipation, turning it on, sitting and watching the blinking cursor as I waited for something to happen. After so much excitement about the advertised possibilities of owning a home computer I sat staring at a blinking cursor in nearly complete disappointment until I discovered the power of the disk.

We've gone from the Industrial Age to the Digital Age in what seems like nanoseconds, and not only has how we access information changed but the values once considered unassailable have crumbled, it seems, almost overnight. The various media forms hold incredible influence over the values of culture with some agendas much more driven than subtle. Values that were once at the fringe of society looking in have now become the dominate values of culture demanding conformity from all. The information age puts all kinds of data at people's fingertips for which many have no interpretive grid to filter out good information from bad, truth-teller from whacko. There was a time when our communities helped us balance truth and falsehood, they helped us recognize the voice of the lunatic fringe but today truth is less important than silencing dissenting opinion, especially those that can't stand the rigors of truthful examination. Today it is not about who is the truest but who is the loudest. The community that once helped us value and discern truth is reduce to the community of social media as I sit in front of my computer all day and never have to interact with a living person. The swamp has changed.

Today we live in a time unlike any other with the possible exception of the first century of the Church. It is a time which presents us with a challenge both for our existence and integrity, and which may ultimately force us to either capitulate to the pressures of a pagan culture or rediscover our Biblical identity as a missionary subculture challenging the values and thinking of our world. We live in a world in which the Church is displaced within the larger culture, and mostly assumed to be innocuous if not redundant or on the more negative side seen as something to be vilified, including Bible believing followers of Jesus Christ.

The Marks of Our Culture:

The Individual is King/Queen: Our world is one of determined individualism, which sets personal preference, whims, and tastes as the ultimate standard for living without any regard to their communal consequences. What once was sin is now just one person's option, as no one would dare say that my "choice" could possibly be wrong lest they be branded as "narrow-minded," "fundamentalist," or "unenlightened." In our individualism we live out our philosophical slogans which in this pre-Christian era have to be neither consistent within or logical without.

I was talking recently to one of the people in our church who mentioned he was taking a course offered by a local school on logic. I suggested that it was a dinosaur that our culture has no interest in but to the credit of whoever is teaching it, their desire is to teach young people how to think critically and use logic. GOD BLESS THEM FOR TRYING!

Arguments today only have to sound good. In reality, many people adopt slogans for living which have ear appeal, but which never have to be scrutinized to see if they are verifiable or logically consistent. Our world is the Star Wars world where the Jedi Knight counsels the young Anakin Skywalker not to "think but feel." We live amid a whole generation of young people who have learned to live not by the exercise of reason but by what feels right, where arguments are from exceptions not the rules, from extremes not the logical, from visual, emotional associations not rational consistency, and where truth becomes trivialized into "whatever works for you."

The Un-Social Media: The wonder of instant access to information is also a wonder in terms of instant access to people through things like social media, Skype, email, Twitter, ZOOM, and texting. All of which has supposedly made us more connected, but the truth is it may very well have made us more isolated. Through the worst of COVID people discovered ZOOM as a means to connect but across the board everyone also discovered it is a poor substitute for actual face to face relationships. Emoticons and avatars are used to express ourselves because of the absence of real time, face to face communication where words are only part of the medium of communication. Studies are now showing that instead of being better connected we are actually more isolated, more disconnected from each other, more distracted than attentive. Social/relational skills become increasingly extinct because we don't have to deal with live people anymore, and we have seen since COVID an increase in the number of people struggling with different forms of mental illness.

What has become clear is that social media has given rise to a whole host of anonymous critics who know no restraint when tearing people down or the kind of hatred and abuse they fling freely without signing their names.

Ask people in retail today what it is like dealing with customers and you'll hear about narcissistic, entitled people who treat those providing customer service with such a level of not only disrespect but contempt that you would have to believe grace, courtesy, and respect died with the dodo bird.

Watch the people in a restaurant the next time you are there and see how many people can't get through a meal without attending to their phones. They may be present to the person on the other end of the phone but absent in real time from the person across the table. "Hello! Can you hear me now?"

Real-Time Emptiness: We live in a world focused on flash, not finish, image not character, all expressing itself in a self-preoccupied stride into emptiness and isolation. It just seems that no matter how far up the ladder we get, no matter how many awards we accumulate, no matter how much money is in the bank, no matter how many toys we accumulate we still can't find contentment with what we have or who we are. A friend has often said, "Never base your identity on something you can lose!" Wise words for this generation.

Our personal preferences, though waved under the banner of freedom in our culture, have actually imprisoned us in our selfish drive for endless satisfactions, mindless entertainment, mounting accumulation of stuff, all emphasizing the emptiness within isolating ourselves from each other and from our communities as we do. Our busy lives don't leave time for people as we pursue our career goals. The values we live isolate us because there are no longer any shared values to act as common ground for living or as protection from our own self-centered existence. Communities have become places where people live and work but where relational networks become increasingly superficial and fragile.

Long days at work mean that most people can barely manage to maintain their relationships with their spouse and children let alone anyone else. In the vacuum of communal values, we struggle to find answers to the problems of violence, crime, child abuse and neglect, and a whole host of cancers that eat away at our cities individually and corporately. We decry the rampant violence in our major cities yet perpetuate a generation of fatherless youth struggling in poverty. Our rugged individualism and relative values have given rise to a "no-fault" society. For example, when tens of thousands of people were infected with HIV from tainted blood products there is no single person or group held culpable. Instead "the system" got blamed. The system takes on a life of its own apparently without accountability or human responsibility, allowing us to abdicate all personal responsibility by saying "the system failed."

Fear and Hopelessness: From 9/11 to hate crimes to mass murders to the war in Ukraine to the conflict in Gaza we are reminded how much our world has changed and how the things we never dreamed could happen in our communities are now happening all the time, sometimes from people radicalized by others sometimes by people neglected and untreated by our communities. Our fear drives us to insulation in our attempts to protect ourselves and ones we love. As more home invasions take place more homes become fortresses. As the tide of violence rises closer to our doorsteps we retreat to our safe havens. Yet what do we find in these so-called safe havens but families and people who are increasingly dysfunctional and broken. Our individualism and subsequent isolation leave us alone in a world whose purpose and meaning are nearly totally derived from ourselves, where we must make our way as "successfully' as possible.

So, what do we do when we lose our job or our marriage, which may be our reason for living? We then struggle with the issues of self-esteem, the meaning of life, and our significance in the world amidst the flotsam and jetsam of life, which too often concludes with the answer of suicide. What do we do when our teen joins a gang or heads to school with hidden weapons? We see him expressing his individuality and though we may have concerns we, nonetheless, permit him to "choose" his option of social or a-social expression.

When another high school shooting takes place what do we do? We say it is a problem of another individual gone wrong deflecting responsibility away from our responsibility in our homes and community. We've lost what our African community has known for a long time, that it takes a village to raise a child. We never say that it is a result of a society which has rendered life meaningless and hopeless by its trivialization of both life and truth. We say it's a problem of upbringing or background deflecting our societal responsibility away from our choices for the values of our communities and so we enact legislation to get guns out of the hands of children. We treat offenders as aberrations from our otherwise good homes and communities, yet those who shoot, and kill come from every strata of society.

Doubt: We also live in a world of cynicism. The failure of humanity in the modern era of Western civilization to deliver on its promise of the goodness and potential of humanity to conquer the problems of evil, pain, and suffering, and the subsequent proof of the darkness of the human soul has led to widespread cynicism. Unlike Star Wars, the forces of good don't always defeat the powers of evil in this world. Indeed, at times the power of good seems defenseless today. Consider the landscape of the last century plus; two world wars, a Holocaust, and a less publicized holocaust in the Sudan, the Vietnam war, genocide in Rwanda and Bosnia, untold numbers of military conflicts, coups, and crises, political, financial, and religious scandals. Biological warfare, scorched earth policies, poisoning of Japanese subways, 9/11, ISIS, Hamas, Hezbollah, and the Boko Harams of the world have all bred a wholesale cynicism about man's goodness, and with it the value of truth which infects every avenue of life.

In a world where truth has been trivialized and values have been relativized, culture floats adrift in a sea of competing voices using only the broken compass of self to determine what is right and wrong, appropriate, or inappropriate, healthy or hurtful. It seems the loudest voice wins whether it is truth based or not.

In this context the church has been shoved off into the periphery of life, a less than credible voice in the smorgasbord of choices and perhaps rightly so. Mainline churches have often expressed views inconsistent within themselves and almost indistinguishable from culture itself while evangelical churches have been content to pronounce their judgments without grace or involvement.

As culture has moved in its perpetual march of "progress" the Church has responded either institutionally, motivated by self-preservation of the status quo or even worse, yesterday's status quo, or it has responded unintelligibly with a cacophony of contradictory voices. Churches have responded to the movements of culture typically with either accommodation to the ruling philosophy of the day thus confusing their voice with the other competing social organizations, or they have responded with embattled isolation, constantly retreating while firing guns at a variety of targets.

Unfortunately, the guns have been firing marshmallow bullets for the most part because those churches have removed themselves from the field of battle and therefore fail the credibility test.

As the Church closed out the last millennium and began a new one it finds itself displaced within her broader culture. Not unlike Judah and Jerusalem in the Old Testament, whose passive stance against the tide of sin landed them in Babylon, the Church finds itself in a precarious change point, relegated to the periphery of life, dominated by a larger culture, struggling to find its identity and purpose among competing voices, and wishing they were back in the good old days in Jerusalem. Like Judah we cry out:

"Joy is gone from our hearts; our dancing has turned to mourning. The crown has fallen from our head. Woe to us, for we have sinned! Because of this our hearts are faint, because of these things our eyes grow dim."
Lamentations 5:15-17

Yet it is this context of a precarious change point which may prove to be the greatest day of the Church. From this swamp we may once again become "the Church," not an institution but a movement, a counter-culture revolution that positively transforms individuals, cities, and nations. From the ruins the Church may once again discover its missionary nature in its encounter with our world and rediscover her God-given priorities, which sift gold from wood and straw, the truly essential from the non-essential.

From the ruins the Church needs to discover afresh the veracity and power of God's Word to change lives, direct ministry, and bring healing to a broken world. From these ruins the Church will need to rediscover its prophetic voice, living and speaking the truth into a culture that has dismissed it but desperately needs it. While culture floods the senses with the messages and images perpetuating individualism, isolation, insulation, and cynicism the Church in in these ruins can influence one life at a time with messages, images and experiences of wholesome, life-giving grace and truth. The church needs to be a part of rebuilding ancient ruins, restoring places long devastated (like human hearts), renewing ruined cities, as the prophet Isaiah foretold in Isaiah 61:4.

Our world is filled with people who are struggling to find meaning and purpose for living, hope in the midst of despair, healing for their brokenness, a sense of community: a sense of belonging to something bigger than they are, a sense of significance: wanting to know that their lives make a difference, and for peace in a turbulent world. Where will they find these needs met? Who will model integrated, whole, purposeful, and significant life for them? The followers of Jesus can, but first it will require a recognition that they are missionaries, that they are not at home anymore but sojourners living in occupied territory and secondly, it will require a right hearing of God's plan for them which results in right action. False prophets are in abundance who will tell us we are not in exile or that we do not need to change or that we just need to be more flexible with our culture, or that if just follow this program, use this strategy, attend this seminar, show this video then things will get better. Those messages give false hope when what we really need are more surrendered lives and churches.

TODAY'S CHALLENGE: Today Christians will need to re-learn the lessons of the Book of Acts, the record of early believers in a missionary encounter with their world; the lessons of Jeremiah, refocusing the exiled people of God on the will of God; and the lessons of Daniel in his successful integration of his faith into his life in a hostile culture. This is the challenge and opportunity being presented to the Church and Christians today; to be in a missionary encounter with our culture, to be the kind of correctable, inspiring, life-giving counterculture which demonstrates the truth and lives credibly through the power of the Holy Spirit before the world. Let's be clear. This is no small task and will require from many of us an almost complete re-orientation of our understanding of what it means to be "the Church" and what it means to be "Christian" in our present cultural climate. It is to that end we now apply ourselves.

CHAPTER TWO

RE-KINDLING VISION FOR THE CITY

Psalm 55:11 Destructive forces are at work in the city; threats and lies never leave its streets.

Proverbs 11:11 Through the blessing of the upright a city is exalted, but by the mouth of the wicked it is destroyed.

Oliver Cromwell was at one time faced with a desperate shortage of the precious metals required to make new coins for England. Finding the banks empty, the mines exhausted, and no gold or silver to be found anywhere, he sent the army throughout the country to find some precious metal to mint more coins. Upon the army's empty-handed return, having been unable to find precious metal anywhere in the land, they apologized for not being able to find any except for the precious metal in the statues of the saints standing in the corners of the church. Cromwell is reported to have responded to the soldiers with, "Well melt down the saints and put them into circulation."

In many ways what Cromwell said about the statues, the Lord Jesus could say about his Church today and about individual Christians; that it's time to melt them down and put them into circulation. Too often today Christians have turned their faith into a comfortable spectator sport where faith is passive, something they believe but not something they necessarily live; a religious option as it were satisfying the "spiritual compartment" of life. Consequently, our compartmentalized living as Christians has too often isolated us in our communities to both our individual and corporate detriment. Today as our communities fall deeper and deeper into the pit of violence, brokenness, hatred, and hopelessness, followers of Jesus need to be put back into circulation. We need to rediscover the vision God has for our communities; to think intentionally about God's desire for them and the people who live in them, as well as the redemptive purpose of His church in the midst.

As of 11:54 am today global population will be 8,071,437,450+. 3.4 billion live in unreached people groups with little or no access with the Gospel of Christ and it is estimated that 155,000 people a day die without Christ in their lives. By 2050 it is estimated that the world population will be 9.7 billion with 80% living in Africa and Asia. Every day 155,000 people die without Jesus. As of 12:00 pm today over 51.6 million people will have been born and over 84,000 people have died globally, a figure meaning nothing unless you realize that roughly 80% of all the people who have ever lived are alive today. [2.] According to UNHCR there are 110 million people forcibly displaced worldwide, including 62.5 million internally displaced people, and 36.4 million who are refugees. [3.] Add to that figure the fact that more than 4.3 billion people now live in urban areas, which means over half of the world (55% in 2017) live in urban settings. The UN estimates this milestone event – when the number of people in urban areas overtook the number in rural settings – occurred in 2007. [4.]

Further, we understand that more people have come to Christ and more have given their lives for Christ in the last century than in all the other centuries added together leading to the conclusion that God is not only bringing people into cities around the world, but more are being reached with the gospel than at any other time. According to the 2022 Status of Global Christianity report, Christianity is growing faster in Africa than in any other place in the world and more Christians live there than in any other continent. By 2050, Africa will be home to almost 1.3 billion Christians, while

Latin America (686 million) and Asia (560 million) will both have more than Europe (497 million) and North America (276 million).[5.] It would seem from the evidence that God is doing something significant in our day that involves our cities. So how do we understand the role of the Church in the city in light of what is happening?

Jack Dennison in his 1999 book City Reaching said "At this very moment, 10,000 South Americans are coming to Christ every single day of the week, 140,000 Africans enter the Kingdom month, and 900,000 Chinese become Christians every year. According to the best global research, 165,000 people a day are coming to Christ worldwide." [6.]

To understand our role is to rekindle vision for the city, our cities, and that begins with understanding from the Scriptures something of how God has moved His people in the past to influence their communities. In the first chapter of Acts we get a glimpse of God's strategy for bringing salvation to the people of the cities, beginning with his disciples in Jerusalem and then in ever widening circles in the surrounding areas. In Jesus' ministry we see how he went intentionally to every city, town and village of Judah and Israel with the good news of the Kingdom, how he sent out the seventy-two to various communities to preach the Kingdom, heal the sick, and cast out demons. (Luke 10:1-23) We get a sense of how the gospel of Christ worked out in the lives of these disciples and then later, when persecution broke out, in their exile, as they were scattered to various places. We see how God would not only use them in their scattering but where He had already been preparing hearts, evidenced in the responses they received.

The rekindling of vision for the city began for the disciples in their time spent with Jesus especially after His resurrection. It was at this time Jesus gave instructions about the role of the disciples, set priorities, and gave the mandate to spread the Good News. In Acts 1:1-3 Luke writes:

"In my former book Theophilus, I wrote about all that Jesus began to do and to teach until the day he was taken up to heaven, after giving instructions through the Holy Spirit to the apostles he had chosen.

After his suffering, he showed himself to these men and gave many convincing proofs that he was alive. He appeared to them over a period of forty days and spoke about the kingdom of God."

We are told that after Jesus was raised from the dead, he spent forty days with the disciples, at which time he gave them instructions, many convincing proofs that he was alive, and that he taught them about the kingdom of God.

The Kingdom of God and the City:

If we are going to rekindle a vision for the city we need to come to some understanding of the kingdom of God as it relates to the city or the world and the salvation of God.

1. The kingdom of God is a present, spiritual reality. It is present partially now and fully in the future. It is about the rule of God in the lives of believers; a rule set up by the Holy Spirit, having a tangible expression and consequences in the present and ultimately in His rule over all creation. The kingdom of God is the rule of God established by the Holy Spirit whereby the He indwells believers, sealing, sanctifying, and empowering their ministries exercised in the larger ministry of the Church which also is born, equipped, and empowered for its mission by the Holy Spirit.

John Stott speaks of the kingdom in this way. "It is spread by witnesses not by soldiers, through a gospel of peace, not a declaration of war, and by the work of the Spirit, not by force of arms, political intrigue, or revolutionary violence." [6.] These characteristics remind us that the kingdom of God is expressed here and now, through the instrumentality of human beings empowered by the Holy Spirit; real people engaged in real life, as real witnesses. God's kingdom and rule, though fully realized in the future when Christ returns, cannot be seen as something to be left on the shelf until then nor can it be seen as something that is simply God's to perform. The recognition of the human instrumentality as "kingdom ambassadors" for God has direct implications on our relationship to the community in which we live. Having said this though, we need to hear Stott's caution that the kingdom of God is apolitical. It cannot be identified with any political ideology or party but must instead be seen as transcending all politics while yet having political ramifications in terms of issues of justice, morality, truth, righteousness, and in every other area where kingdom and cultural values clash.

Jesus' method of proclaiming the Gospel was first and foremost incarnation. (Philippians 2:5-8) He came to us and became like us to share life and His life for us. The missionary call on all our lives is to do the same. To become like, to come alongside others, without surrendering our identity and values as Christ-followers so that others might come to know Christ. When we cross cultural barriers, we cross them not to make new Canadians but to make Africans better Africans within their own culture, Asians better Asians within their own culture, First Nations people better First Nations people because of Christ in their lives.

It is precisely at this juncture that we see the challenge of the Church today. Exiled to the periphery of life the values of the kingdom of God are in constant collision with the values of our secular, pre-Christian society. Life is sacred, it would seem, only if you are a dolphin, a whale, or a seal pup, while the lives the unborn, the elderly, the sick, or handicapped are all at grave risk through abortion, euthanasia, or neglect. Morality is today defined by consensus, which in itself is a floating standard, different today than yesterday, and different tomorrow from today, with no fixed reference points. If enough people say loudly enough and long enough that something is right before long culture agrees. The family is re-defined to absurdity so that it becomes any group of people from your workplace to your sports team who demand it, whether different sex or the same, and the home which once was the stable building block of society becomes one of the many dysfunctional wrecks dotting the cultural landscape, left without a map to navigate the treacherous waters of this world.

The values of our post-modern/pre-Christian world flow from some basic assumptions. The first is that we arrive in this world as a fluke, a genetic accident, a freak of nature, having risen out of the primordial slime, evolved as humanity, and therefore having no responsibility to or for anyone but ourselves and no accountability to anyone or anything other than what is "democratically" agreed upon. With this assumption there is no "greater' purpose in life, no ultimate meaning, no rhyme or reason for the chaos we live, and religion is just a crutch for the weaker members, or else some general expression of "spirituality" as an aspect of our "being". In this way the Church is exiled to the periphery of life as just one of the many "spiritual" options a person may choose to guide their lives, as long as we understand that it is all personal and we cannot assert our beliefs on any other person or their exclusive claims of truth.

From this peripheral place the Church must recover its voice and its mission, demonstrating that we have encountered Jesus Christ as the living Saviour, that we have been changed, having had our lives re-oriented to the compass of God's Word and the cross which graciously call us into relationship with the Creator who calls us to be responsible people and accountable to Him. When the Church understands that this happens most effectively not with a loud voice nor with spiritual guns blazing but quietly and winsomely as one person at a time is changed and one neighborhood at a time is changed, then we will have begun to have the credibility from which can influence change in the larger community. When the Church takes off its sanctified robes, gets down on its knees and begins to get dirty dealing with the real needs of our communities then people will listen.

Another collision takes place between truth and relativism. Most of our young people today have been weaned in a culture which says everything is relative, that there are no black and whites. As distasteful as it is today to either tell someone they are wrong or admit that we are, we cannot simply ignore the illogic of life built around relativism in the hope it will go away or that someone will eventually have an epiphany. When I go to my doctor with a pain I want him to believe that there is a right answer and a wrong answer, one of which will lead to health and the other of which will not. We all have an interest in truth but ironically, when it comes to lifestyle issues in that arena, we want truth to be something we can conveniently set aside. Is it that we are concerned about fairness and truth or is it that we simply want to legitimize our lifestyle or particular behaviors? Amazingly, in our day an opportunity is afforded Christians to state their case perhaps like few other seasons but we often adopt a reclusive attitude instead. In an age of relativism, the highest value is placed on pragmatic personal story. "If it works for you, great!" We have an opportunity to tell others that Jesus Christ does make a difference in our lives and that faith in God works, but that leads to the next collision.

There is also a collision today in reference to integrity, both personally and corporately as a nation. As a nation we frown on the abuse of human rights, but we refuse to reign in oil companies that perpetuate loss of life in the Sudan. We cry out against child pornography but see no inconsistency in allowing other forms for ourselves. We mourn the loss of innocent children gunned down in our schools but share no responsibility for violent behaviors permitted in our homes through video games, movies, etc. and wonder how such things happen. We see no clash of values when we watch and send athletes to Olympic Games hosted by nations known for their human rights violations instead of boycotting them to send the message that no amount of money or entertainment can substitute for the loss of human rights and lives.

The lack of personal integrity in our day is reflected corporately in the number of political and business scandals. We hear of investigations into mutual fund dealers who at the end of the term do what they can to inflate the value so that over the long run it "appears" better to the investor. We read about bit coin entrepreneurs whose primary value seems to have been filling their own pockets at the expense of others. We hear of the moral failures of leaders in almost every realm of life, including the Church.

Issues of integrity show up in the minutiae of life, whether it is not returning the $10, $20, or $50 we find left behind in the instant teller machine, rationalizing it on the basis of the exorbitant profits the banks are making anyways, or whether it is the liberating of supplies from the office for our homes, or the host of personal secrets we keep about the person we are in private as opposed the one we are in public.

There is an orientation of mind that says, "If I can get away with it, if it doesn't seem to hurt anyone, then, why not do it?" In our city people run red lights like the colour doesn't matter. Why? In a "me first" world if I can, I will. I went down to the local Taco Bell one day for lunch and lined up behind about six young people probably of university age.

Because I was standing close it was hard not hear what they ordered, a soft taco and a glass of water. When they got their cups, they went to the fountains and filled them .... with pop and I thought to myself that it's a small thing, but it tells me a lot about the integrity of those six individuals. My conclusion was that if I couldn't trust them to take the glass of water, they asked for rather than the soda pop they didn't pay for, then I'm certainly not going to trust them with the larger matters of life.

The struggle for integrity is not just in the world but even in the lives of believers where it is doubly problematic as individual compromises of integrity affect the integrity of the whole body. If our integrity isn't intact, our credibility and witness for Christ are also tainted.

In the collision of values taking place today our world pulls us away from those things that allow us to live at peace with ourselves and our communities, and then we act shocked when people take their valueless world to its logical conclusion in crime, murder, insider trading, suicide, genocide, and "scandals" of every description. Yet the call of God is to live integrated lives of value, with values that flow from being created for a purpose. It is to live Christ-centered lives.

In the Willowbank Report produced by the Lausanne Committee on World Evangelism this is what they say about the Christ-centred life:

"Jesus insists on dislodging from the centre of our world whatever idol previously reigned on the throne." [8.]

When we look at the collision of values between the kingdom of God and post-current society, would we not say with Cromwell, "It's time to melt down the saints and put them into circulation."

Being a kingdom ambassador is to be a witness for Jesus Christ and the values of His kingdom. When Jesus rose to the right hand of the Father, he called his disciples to be his witnesses in their home town, their province, their neighboring province, and around the world, to the people they had the most in common with and with those with whom they had the least, to the people they loved most and the people they hated most. They would be his instruments by which the message of liberty and salvation would be translated into the lives of others.

The kingdom of God is a present spiritual reality that has practical ramifications for everyday living right now. As Christians are melted down and put into circulation the credibility of their witness increases in their communities.

2. The kingdom of God, as not yet fully consummated, calls us to a forward progress. In this "now' but "not yet fully" component the Church and Christians are reminded that once we are saved the work is not over but just beginning. We are called to be a counterculture within the larger culture, engaging it on its own terms and challenging every thought and pretense that sets itself up against God and his Word. We are ambassadors of Kingdom policy and foot-soldiers of the cross, all rolled into one.

A few years ago, the Canadian Legion decided to take a stand over headwear in response to Sikh members who could not remove their turbans without becoming religiously defiled. Not so long ago it didn't matter what soldiers wore when they stood on the battlefield and fought to push back a common enemy. How quickly, once the fire of battle dies down do we forget the freedom purchased and begin to erect walls to separate us!

The issue reminds me of many churches which dissolve or worse implode over internal matters that are far from world shaking or even, dare I say it, important. We find the strangest things to disagree about with one another, from where we sit on Sunday, to what songs we sing, to how we worship, to what the dimensions of the offering envelope should be. I once sat in on an annual meeting of a church where a friend was moderating the meeting and listened to them pass a million-dollar budget in five minutes and then argue for half an hour over the format of the offering envelope. We get into tiffs over whether the young couples should be able to use the church van for their retreat, and who makes the final decisions officially and unofficially.

People divide and conquer over church trivialities, get mired in institutional swamplands, while the world looks in wondering why the church, which is supposed to be such a wellspring of life, always seems to be such a harsh environment for living. For a community from which one might expect more hope and inspiration it sure seems to be more often a like group of religious museum curators wrestling over who gets to hold the relics.

We've travelled a longways from Jesus' day, but it hasn't always been forward. Movement is not necessarily progress. The movement of the Church to the periphery within our culture has not been a result of a thorough engagement with it but a result of distancing from it, resulting in a fractured voice and scandalized image. As a people of the kingdom of God there is a call on our lives to become re-acquainted with the King's policies and practices, to shed the soiled garments of self-centeredness, and to live real lives as real people in a real world.

Similarly, to the disciples of Jesus there is a need for a correction of perception. In those forty days where Jesus taught and no doubt, answered many questions he was asked: "Lord, are you at this time going to restore the kingdom to Israel?" The phrase "at this time" suggests that the disciples were looking for a kingdom that was immediately curative and restorative, negating the amount of work they would have to do, and the amount of learning that would be required of them.

It is the age-old quest for God to do all the work while we await the rewards, not unlike many Christians today waiting for God to "save" our land as we sit watching and waiting for signs of that movement.

Yet if Jesus did "restore" the kingdom at that time how would the disciples ever overcome things like the racism displayed in John 4 with the Samaritan woman, in the Samaritan revival of Acts 8 with Peter and Cornelius in Acts 10. Owning our flaws is painful but usually the best way to learn from them so as to not repeat them is to go through the pain. The word "restore" suggests that they really had not yet grasped the nature of the kingdom Jesus was bringing, a present reality and fully consummated in the future. They were still looking for a "political" solution for their social and religious ills, for Israel to be restored as a national kingdom expressive of God's rule and vindicated before the occupying nation. At this point it was appropriate for some correction of perception from Jesus.

As the Church today slowly recognizes its estrangement and seeks to regain "power" through the political process it needs similar correction which comes from seeing things from God's perspective, from listening to Jesus' teaching as it relates to our cities, and instituting His values in our lives, our communities, our workplaces, and our schools. It is time for the people of God to be put back into circulation, to get out of the fortress and come alive because if we do not our cities and our nation will continue on its path of self-destruction.

We need to recognize that our re-emergence into the world is not most effective when we seek to use political means. There are many Christians today who simply want to have returned the institutional power the church once held in society so it can legislate right morality, values etc. Unfortunately, when the church has held "power" it has not always had a very good track record and has tended towards abuse of power. We ought also to learn from the mistakes of our Muslim friends who in seeking to institute an Islamic society by law and power have created a rebound effect among their own people which has led many to turn to Christ instead. A political response alone has all the earmarks of Jonah's compassionless ministry in Nineveh. We do well to remember that while the kingdom of God has political implications it is to be apolitical.

The kind of correction required of us is one that recognizes that we are a part of the problem in our communities and that our communities and nation are not just vulgar commodities but real people, people with whom we live, work, and play. At that point where we begin to recognize sin for what it is and recover compassion for sinners, like us, rather than the thundering judgment we have perfected, we may begin to regain credibility. At that point where we begin to live again with enough integrity to be able to handle the delicate balance between recognizing sin yet loving the sinner, we may begin to have a restorative influence. It is time to see cities as people in need of something we have to offer.

Jesus' response to the disciple's question was essentially a dismissal of it and a challenge instead to pay more attention to more pressing matters. Then, as He is lifted up before them, as they gaze intently up into the sky, an interesting question is posed by the two men dressed in white: "Why do you stand here looking into the sky?" as if to say: Don't you have something you're supposed to be doing?"

Herein lies the rub for the Church. It is much easier to stand looking at past ministry than to engage in real ministry today. We might want to examine ourselves to see if we have become too enamored with the politics of religion and the nation either in the solutions we seek for our communities or in our maintenance of the "institution." I recently heard from a friend who has been doing excellent, life-giving ministry in a rural church for years. This is a church for which the district leadership could not find a pastor until he was asked to supply in the void. He is now being asked by the denomination of the congregation to step down because of differing views about baptism, something that has not been an issue for the congregation. Let me be clear, I am not against theological integrity, but when you have someone providing life-giving ministry where no one else was willing to do it I'd like to think I'd choose the life-giving ministry over the ministry void. He wrote:

"The church leadership team has been a blessing to me, the denomination itself has expressed its appreciation for the work I have done, and their regret that they will have to remove me because of denominational policy.

At best this seems to me to be a short-sighted view of the Kingdom of God and at its worst denominational and institutional insecurity that will perpetuate denominational decline. They could have a healthy rural church that is life-giving in their district, or they can act in such a way as to lose a healthy congregation over their institutional stance. Again, I'm not saying that churches should not be interested I theological integrity, but I am saying that a little tolerance on non-essentials from the institution can allow for life in a local congregation to grow without outside incumbrances and be a blessing to their community.

On the other hand, we easily become preoccupied with the heavenly Jesus, vacantly staring into the sky awaiting His return and the solution to all our problems.

To some degree we have probably been guilty of both, and both have contributed to a false sense of security as we have entrusted our responsibility socially to the politicians and religiously to the professional clergy. The result usually has been some new program of education or something similar as we watch from the sidelines. Both have contributed to a false piety, one where faith is detached from faithful action. We might legitimately be asked "Why are you standing here looking up, isn't there something you are supposed to be doing?" The most basic reality is that until Jesus comes again to consummate his kingdom, we have work to do, a mission to fulfill, people to be healed. It is an immense task, yet as our perceptions are adjusted, as we learn from Jesus by attending to His Word and are attentive to the Holy Spirit, it can be done.

When Jesus dismissed the question of the disciples, He also gave them a commission; to be his witnesses in Jerusalem, Judea, Samaria, and the ends of the earth. As immense as the task is, to be Jesus' witnesses, we are not left to fulfill it by our ingenuity, intelligence, nor by our own abilities, though they may all factor in, but we are empowered by the Holy Spirit for the task.

In verse 8 Jesus said to the disciples,

> *"But you will receive power when the Holy Spirit comes on you; and you will be my witnesses in Jerusalem....."*

To be ambassadors for the kingdom of Christ requires the active dynamism of the Holy Spirit working within us, molding, shaping, guiding, directing, and empowering us, lest we lapse back into false activism and or false piety. The disciples were not told at this point to head for the hills but to go back to their city.

The Matthew 28 commissioning relates the making of disciples of all nations to this task which would begin in Jerusalem. Even at that time God was gathering people from the nations into Jerusalem in anticipation of the Pentecost celebration. Only God could arrange such events.

For years after I came to Christ, I wanted to serve in missions and yet as hard as I pursued it the more fragile was my equilibrium of peace within. Eventually I realized God didn't want me on the "mission field" as much as I did, and that my calling was here in Canada.

Growing up in Cape Breton I had learned to despise Ontario because it represented everything economically and otherwise, we did not have; a passion that was particularly expressed in hatred for Toronto. In an interesting twist in God's sense of humor this Jonah found himself pastoring a church in his Nineveh (Toronto), one of the most cosmopolitan cities of the world. I found myself pastoring in a location where God had brought the world to my doorstep, and I was now being challenged to stop looking at the sky and look at the nations all around me. God began to knit my heart to the city, and I began to see that He was giving me an opportunity to be a "missionary" right here.

God is still calling His witnesses today. For some it is to go to the farthest reaches of the globe but for most it may be right where we are living now. In places like Toronto God has brought the world to our doorstep, but Toronto is not alone. Around the world today God is bringing more and more people from their rural settings increasingly into cities. The urbanization and internationalizing of our cites is a reality we must grasp if we will see God's kingdom in our cities. We must have a view of God and our world that is large enough to see what He is doing and respond accordingly.

In 1970 there were less than 70 megacities (cities with over 10,000,000 people). In 2015 there were 463. [9.] God is bringing people together into cities, exiles from their "home" lands, often isolated and alone within ours. The Church needs to rediscover its role in hospitality to the weak, weary, helpless, and hopeless among us. We need to remember we are sojourners in this world, travelers who have much in common with the "refugees" in our cities, a people of tents not power and status, who are moving toward a heavenly destination, and who have learned to cling to the things of this "city" lightly. We need to know who the people are living around us and find ways to build bridges. It is time to stop pulling up the draw bridge and get out of the castle.

Ray Bakke tells the story of the city of Belgrade on the drug route from Turkey with its large drug problem. At one time the Marxist government offered the churches a building and funds to run a drug rehabilitation centre, which they refused because they did not know how to cope with it and did not want to. [10.] Our cities testify to the lack of desire on the part of churches to cope with the urban problems of the day. It is born out in parochial attitudes of non-cooperation with other churches, in the lack of united prayer for our cities, in leaders who are trained to maintain institutions rather than direct mission outposts, in ghettoized self-absorbed Christianity which would rather fight over worship songs than deal with the neglect and death of our cities' children and homeless.

What we thought was morally impossible twenty-five years ago has happened today, and what we think impossible today may very well happen in the next fifteen. Sin is undefinable in any meaningful terms for our society today. With a floating standard of morality how long will it be before all the fences are down and everything goes?

In the Gandhi movie a scene plays itself out where the political leaders of India and Pakistan are meeting to determine whether there will be one nation united or two in tension with each other. Gandhi recognized that if the two religious factions could not live in harmony together in one nation then as two they would simply be at "war" with each other constantly and he asked those leaders a question something like, "Will you build the kind of India your children can be proud of?" The wisdom of his evaluation and question have been born in evidence of how the two nations have related to each other since. Gandhi's question is a real one for us today as well.

The questions I ask myself are these: Is this the kind of Canada, the kind of city I can be proud of and want to reside in? Am

I the kind of Christian I should be in this cultural climate? Is my congregation the kind of mission outpost it is supposed to be?

Our choices are three: Flight - We can run away from the problems to a new "cleaner and safer" environment hoping the problems don't follow us. Fight - We can resist the changes that are happening around us hoping instead to outlast them until the other side comes around. (Don't hold your breath!) or we can throw in our lot to Fix it. The choice of the people of God ought to be to stand up, to make a difference in Jesus name and for the sake of the people who are dying all around us without Christ. It seems to me that the people most involved in turning around local economies, helping the poor and homeless, tackling corrupt institutions, and making the community a better place to live should be the Christians, that is if we truly believe in the power of God to make a difference. Because of Christ we have hope, we believe things can change by God's grace and people and communities with them.

We have a gospel that can change the broken, distorted, hopeless lives around us while restoring the health of the community. At stake are our families, our neighborhoods, our cities, and our nation. It is time for a fresh expression of Kingdom life and wholeness by the Church to meet the need of the hour. It's time for the saints to be melted down and put into circulation.

ENDNOTES

1. http://www.worldometers.info/world-population/

2. http://www.worldometers.info/world-population/#total

3. https://www.unhcr.org/refugee-statistics/

4. https://ourworldindata.org/urbanization

5. https://research.lifeway.com/2022/01/31/7-encouraging-trends-of-global-christianity-in-2022/

6. Jack Dennison - City Reaching, pg. 9

7. John Stott - Commentary on the Acts of the Apostles

8. The Willowbank Report –

9.https://www.statista.com/topics/4841/megacities/#topicOverview

10. Ray Bakke - The Urban Christian pg. 59

CHAPTER THREE

PUTTING DOWN ROOTS

Jeremiah 29:5
"Build houses and settle down.."

We live in what is now referred to as the post-modern era. I prefer to call it a pre-Christian era. As the post-modern name indicates it is after the modern era but also it marks the end of the era of Christendom, where the Church functioned as a powerful influence and shaper of life. I'd like to suggest that we live not just in the post-modern era but maybe more appropriately in the disposable era.

If you look around you find that almost everything in sight, one way or another, is considered disposable by us today. You find that diapers are disposable, razors are disposable, drinking containers are disposable, noodle containers are disposable, pens are disposable, cameras are disposable, your coffee pods and dinner china can be disposable, and your cutlery with it. Look around and you'll see a world that's full of disposable items, fueling the landfill crisis in most urban jurisdictions.

One of the things that strikes me increasingly in our culture is that people and relationships are increasingly being considered disposable as well. In the last number of years we see people treating each other as disposable in terms of relationships over values and beliefs on things from vaccines to politics to social values. It's one thing to disagree on those subjects but more recently if someone disagrees with you on the smallest detail that person often then becomes the enemy. Hatred is so easy!

When you talk to teachers in our schools today you talk to people who are confronted everyday with school boards pressing an agenda that divides families within schools, teaching values that deepen the loss of a solid foundation for life for children. In the absence of a belief in God humanity now sits on the throne accountable to no one. The issues of brokenness in our children gets perpetuated rather than healed, even though we increasingly recognize that our children are suffering mentally and emotionally.

Consider those children coming to school from homes where parents are constantly fighting with each other. Consider the number that are abused either verbally or physically, who too often have little to no sense of worth or esteem. The nurturing of a nation's children has been turned over to the state as both parents work for the "good" life and others raise their children with non-neutral state/cultural values.

When we started the church plant from our Orleans church fifteen minutes down the Ottawa River in Rockland, one of the corner pieces of our outreach was a Friday night youth drop in. I remember one Friday evening as parents were coming to pick up their teenagers that there was a comment on teen behavior in terms of trying to get them to do what they are asked from one of the parents who essentially summed up his perspective by saying, "O well, she's not my kid!"

In other words, because the family was blended, he wasn't going take responsibility for this particular child. I remember how my heart broke within me when I heard those words and as I thought about what that child's tender heart would learn in that familial relationship about her value and worth.

In a strike of Support Staff of the Toronto School Board a frustrated parent was quoted as saying he thought the schools should be deemed an "essential service" and not be permitted to close because people like him and his wife both work, making the closing of the schools a real hardship. I understand what he was saying and the hardship he and his wife face in times like strikes and snow days but I found myself sitting in disbelief that an "enlightened" Canadian, assumedly educated should miss the point so badly. We make choices about the lifestyle we want to live and when it works out with the help of the free childcare provided by our schools everything is fine, but let's be clear about what is an "essential service." It is not the free childcare provided by our schools. An essential service is, however, parenting. Increasingly we see our schools shaping the values of students that was once the domain of families and even to the point recently where families having different values than the current school values may feel the censure of the government. Children need their parents to love them by nurturing them, setting the standard for the values to be lived out, modelling it, and by teaching them. Schools are only as essential as parents choose to make them. The family in Jeremiah's model was the influencer of community not the other way around.

In our culture women give birth to children they don't want and abandon them in dumpsters or public washrooms. Adoption is near impossible because of the number of abortions, and the sick and elderly are at the mercy of the philosophy governments who now dictate to doctors the determination as to what is "viable" life.

Euthanasia now becomes not so much an act of mercy as it is driven by economics and perspective of life. If your marriage isn't what you dreamed it would be you can dispose of it through divorce and dissolution as a simple solution requiring the least amount of effort, and for those who live together in common-law there is always the option of walking away when you live in a disposable relationship.

People treat life so cheaply that they settle disputes with guns and knives. Teens kill teens with little thought about much more than their own thoughts of revenge or greed. We are reaping in our culture and in our time the fruit of attitudes which treat all of life as if it is disposable. Unless something changes children growing up now, having been raised in the disposable age, will bear unknown fruit in days to come, perhaps in ways we would find unimaginable now, simply because so many of these children have been raised with values that can't support life. The experience of a functional, whole family and home increasingly becomes a fiction rather than a fact and we find ourselves living in a very difficult and different day, and yet that is God's model for showing the world what healthy relationships can look like. Where the family fails it then falls on the church to model those healthy relationships.

Mission Strategy for Today's Church:

Step 1 - Put Down Roots.

When Judah was carried off into captivity, in many ways their destination as far as they were concerned was a disposable land. When Nebuchadnezzar in 597 BC took roughly three thousand people captive from Judah and Jerusalem, including the king, the royal household, all the people who were acquainted with all the finer arts, and everything of any value in Judah depositing them in Babylon, the Judean exiles found themselves living in a land that was very different.

It was also for them a very difficult transition. They found themselves living in an ungodly, a hostile land, as they considered it, among barbarians. They were stripped of all their creature comforts, ripped away from their homes and the Temple, which was the centre of life and religion, and as far as they were concerned, they were alone, abandoned by God. Yet, in the midst of all this, in the context of their exile in captivity God gives to the people of Judah a missionary call.

The missionary call is this, *"build houses and settle down, plant gardens and eat what they produce, marry and have sons and daughters, find wives for your sons and give you daughters in marriage so that they too may have sons and daughters, increase in number there, do not decrease."*

Let me suggest three descriptions of the missionary call found here. The missionary call to Judah came with an open time frame. It came with freedom and finally, the missionary call came when the harvest season was ripe in Babylon. It may be that as the Church today learns from its own past it may be able to rediscover its own mission and purpose in its cultural context.

The Missionary call came with an open time frame.

The first part of the mission strategy for the exiles is heard in the word from God given to Jeremiah for Judah in captivity, "Put down roots!" When the captives were escorted away obviously one of the questions on the mind of the people had to do with how long they were liable to be in captivity. The false prophets were telling everyone this captivity was going to be short. 'So, don't unpack your suitcases, don't get ready for a long stay, we're only going to be here a short time', was precisely the message Judah and the exiles wanted to hear. They didn't want to stay in Babylon. They didn't want to be with these foreigners, these barbarians. That was a good word from the Lord as far as they were concerned because it gave them the answer they were looking for, the answer they all wanted to hear.

Unfortunately, Jeremiah was getting a different signal from the Lord. He sent a letter to the political expedient of the day, Zedekiah, warning the people that they needed to wait upon the Lord for His timing in the matter, which as it turned out was not a short stay but a prediction of a 70-year sojourn. In essence he told them the Lord was saying, "You're not going to be here for a short time but a long time. Unpack your suitcases!" The Lord was saying, "I know what you want but what you want is not what you need, nor is it what you are going to get. I have something for you to do here, and until you get with the program you're not going anywhere!" God was making these exiles, these captives, missionaries to the Babylonians. His word to them is put down roots, build homes for yourselves, settle down.

What Judah needed to understand was something of the timing and the purposes of God if they were going to fulfil their missionary purpose in Babylon and it is here that we find the common ground for the church at odds with our culture today.

In order for the exiles to put down roots there were some lessons they needed to learn, the first of which was to learn submission. If they took the word that said they were going to have a short stay, a short captivity, a short exile, it nullified the disciplinary effect of them being taken into captivity. They could sit and endure almost anything for two years and in the process totally miss the point, but if they understood it wasn't Nebuchadnezzar who had taken them into captivity, but as Jeremiah highlights in his letter, it was the Lord who carried them into captivity (vs.4 *"...those I carried into exile."*) then the time spent was of much greater significance. Nebuchadnezzar was only an instrument. God was the actor on this stage. This was not about the ambition of Nebuchadnezzar. It was about seeing God as in control and one who could be trusted even when their lives seemed out of control. The words almost sound like God is saying: "You are where you are not because of some impish ruler you fear but because I, whom you refuse to fear, have deposited you right where I want you." It was only as they understood who was in charge, who was sovereign, that the people of Judah could begin to learn their lesson about submission to the will and the timing of the Lord. Wisdom for Judah was submission and obedience.

How often had God taught them to look beyond the surface? They learned this lesson in the story of Joseph who introduced his brothers to a bigger picture, "What you meant for evil, God intended for good." They learned it in the story of Moses who went from Pharoah's excellence to Midian exile to wilderness expert as the leader of God's people. They heard the echoes of Joshua and Caleb who said "Giants, Schmiants! If God is for us nobody can defeat us!"

How often has God taught us to look beyond the surface. Consider the Babylonian success story of Daniel and his companions as they integrated their faith into a hostile environment. Consider the persecution of the church in Jerusalem which forced it not only to spread the gospel resulting in revival in Samaria but also forced it to deal with its own racism.

Consider Antioch and the first cross cultural ministry which began because people didn't know they were not supposed to share Christ with their neighbors.

Consider Peter's revelation and the Gentile mission to Cornelius and his house. Consider the persecution under the Romans and the spread of the Church, the persecution in China and the fruit now being harvested, the prayer which focused on the eastern bloc countries for decades and the miraculous coming down of the Berlin Wall. How many times must we learn to look beyond the surface?

Part of the problem for Judah, however, was their perception of their captors and their place of captivity. The Babylonian world was a disposable environment in the mind of these exiles. They needed to begin to see that Babylon was not necessarily the unclean nation that they thought it was. They needed to understand that they were not alone, having left the Temple and assumedly the presence of the Lord back in Jerusalem. They needed to understand that God was bigger than that and even more importantly that this was a sacred place because God was there with them and had a purpose for them to fulfil. The lost lesson of submission is that anyplace God's presence calls us to be is better by far than any other place we could ever hope to be, away from His purpose and presence.

If the attitude of the exiles was that Babylon was a disposable environment, then how much more so is it today in the Church which sits on the sidelines waiting for God to intervene in our cities? Even worse is the attitude of calling for fire from heaven in judgement on the sin of our captors while refusing to be light and a leavening influence in the committee and board rooms, the streets and alleys, the parks and malls, the sports teams, gyms, and community centres of our communities.

Judah had some growing up to do, which included getting beyond their prejudices. The tendency for the people of Judah was to consider anyone that was foreign a barbarian. Their first consideration of them was as scum who made you unclean ceremonially just by contact with them, let alone the host of cultural suitcases full of prejudice they carried with them. They were grieved at the prospect of rubbing elbows with Babylonians every day because they had a holy God who at head of their nation said to them "I am holy, you also be holy." They did not comprehend that there was little more barbaric in the eyes of God than one who knows the truth yet spurns it. Though they were blind to their own unholiness which had landed them in this mess, they could still use the pretense of holiness to reinforce their stereotypes of others to elevate themselves.

They needed, instead, to understand that the Babylonians and Nebuchadnezzar were not the villains in this drama, but their precise predicament was a result of their own actions. They had been warned time and time again to pay attention to their relationship to God, but they opted for neglect instead, for what was in vogue religiously in their time. Their situation in Babylon could only be redeemed if it would cause them to lift their eyes to heaven and acknowledge their sin. The discipline of God was being enacted through Nebuchadnezzar and it would be a success only if they repented.

Their submission would begin when they acknowledged they were out of control, that Nebuchadnezzar and the Babylonians were not the villains and that their sin was the cause of their circumstances. They needed to see that they were to be God's instruments for reaching the Babylonians and causing them to lift their eyes to heaven.

In their consideration of being holy they recognized there were some things that made you unclean and one of those things was being in the fellowship of the wrong people. The faults of the Babylonians loomed much larger in their eyes than did their own abandonment of God.

The early church struggled with the same issue when they had to determine in the Jerusalem Council whether you had to be a circumcised to be a Christian, in other words was it possible to be a Gentile Christian without being Jewish. Ironically, in the church today many people think the reverse; that a Jew, in order to be a Christian has to stop being Jewish. Thankfully the Jerusalem Council remembered the wonder of grace and figured out that it is all about our relationship to Jesus not the law.

Judah in its legalistic expression of holiness had long since lost sight of God, a blindness that would restrict them in their ability to consider the missionary call of God upon their lives as leavening influences wherever they were placed, and that's exactly what God was doing in Babylon. He was calling the people of Judah to be a leavening influence, a redeeming influence upon the nation of Babylon. To do so they had to overcome their worldview, that Babylon and Babylonians were the enemy, and that they were not exactly the plaid rabbit themselves.

They needed to realize that if God was present with them in Babylon, then Babylon was a sacred place; the same lesson that Moses learned in reference to the burning bush. It was holy ground not because the bush was on fire but because God was there, and Judah needed to understand that God was in Babylon with them. He had called them to that place, he had a purpose for them to perform, He was with them not absent, and graciously waiting for them to look to Him and return. It was time for them to take their eyes off themselves and begin to see the opportunity that God had presented them.

If ever there is to be hope for our city it will be when the people of God begin to realize they are in a place God has carried them, where they do not have the luxury of squabbling over what songs to sing, who serves the communion, or whether the pastor visits them or not. Exile reduces life to simplicity in the extreme:

learn submission and see tomorrow or do otherwise to your own detriment.

There are lessons to be learned by the Church in our context today about the recognition of who is in control, even when we think we have got it all together, lessons about recognizing the instruments God uses to discipline and challenge us, and lessons about our own sin/failings which have landed us where we did not choose to be. I believe God has a plan for our churches where they are rooted to give life to their communities, no matter how big or small.

In our present disposable age, we cannot permit ourselves to be cast aside, relics of yesterday, to become religious museums deemed irrelevant today at the whim of our culture but must rediscover our missionary purpose under God. The Church exists in every generation to reach its own generation with the gospel of Jesus Christ. In Acts 13:36 it says this about King David,

> *"Now when David had served God's purpose*
> *in his own generation,*
> *he fell asleep;"*

It is a reminder that God has a Kingdom purpose for us in every generation. The Church is not a fortress intended as a hiding place, a refuge for saints. It is not a mirror which reflects its culture. It is the Bride of Christ, radiant and winsome for her generation, a credible witness to the truth and power of the gospel. The Church in every generation exists as a credible witness only as it lives with integrity in its missionary encounter with the world.

There is no credibility in the postures of accommodation to culture or isolation from it. It is only as the Church adapts to the changed world around it by relating the timely and timeless message of the eternal truths of God to the everyday dysfunctionality of sin that we begin to have credibility. There is an urgency today to see that our Babylon is not an enemy prison camp, but an opportunity presented to us by God; that the Babylonians with whom we live are not the enemy but hurting, needy, broken people to whom God has brought us, and for whom Christ has died. We need to begin to consider our neighborhoods, our workplace, the clubs where we go to exercise, not as disposable environments but environments to be redeemed by Jesus Christ through us. In other words, to put down roots, not run away and hide.

Our cities today seem to consist of disposable communities. A disposable community is one where we give ourselves permission to leave because it seems either hopeless or too much work to change. When we look around and say I don't like this neighborhood, this neighborhood is bad, the people are bad, or I don't like living in this neighborhood and move to another, we create another disposable neighborhood. The history of urban centres is that people move from downtown to ever broadening circles farther away. They move farther out, constantly mobile, constantly moving from one disposable neighborhood to another often in response to who is moving in, yet what happens when the good people leave a neighborhood or feel it's too much work to make it better?

These days in Canada there is a housing crisis where the people who feel it most are the new immigrants and refugees who have been granted entry but for whom there are no homes, no places to stay and therefore no work because they don't have a fixed address. How long will it be before their desperation falls prey to darker elements. There is never a vacuum for long, something always fills it and usually it is not for the better.

Our youth pastor told us of a visit to Chicago a few years ago where another youth pastor showed him the housing projects in area where he was working. He took them to some large housing towers and showed them one particular tower where the two top floors were darkened out because the gangs owned them. They never paid anything for them, they just took them over. They owned them by occupation, they put down roots, and they are now rule of the day in those neighborhoods.

A young woman was interviewed on the news here a month ago about a shooting in her building complex. "O, its normal around here!"

God forbid that people getting shot and killed in our communities should ever become "normal" for us!

Another woman was interviewed in reference to three murders which have taken place over two week period. In the interview she talked about how gangs had seemingly taken over her neighborhood because good people were doing nothing, with her final comment on the whole situation being that it was time for the good people to reclaim the community. Unfortunately, the reality is that as long as good people move out of their communities, they are not going to reclaim anything.

How does it happen? It happens when we have disposable neighborhoods, when the good people say I don't like it here anymore and leave, and all the leavening influences, all the redeeming influences are removed with them. What's going to happen in our cities if we perpetuate disposable neighborhoods, if crime is left as a police or government problem? The violence, the crime, will only escalate. When the light is removed only darkness grows. When sin is lifted up and elevated from the bottom as something good, virtue is necessarily brought low as something less than great and desirable and we all suffer. In this light I applaud the Move In Ministry where people intentionally move into difficult areas of cities so that they can be a redeeming influence by their presence and the relationships they build.

The lesson for Judah was to put down roots. Their missionary call came with an open time frame. They had the time to do what they needed. They needed to learn that God was going to give them time, two generations worth, to both learn submission and impact their world. They were going to need to unpack the suitcases and make a commitment to living there, staying there, being a people involved in the city. If we have concerns for our cities in crisis, then we have to be committed to staying where that mission call has been given to us, to be all that we can be for Jesus' sake in the community and for the sake of our children. In the absence of good people - God's people, everything goes. When the leaders in morality, responsibility, mutual concern for one another, and brotherly love are extinguished in the community, only the weeds of hatred, prejudice, bigotry, violence, and abuse grow. What we need are more flowers- the people of God; people who know Jesus Christ as their Lord and Saviour, who understand the power of God's love to transform lives, who understand the power of forgiveness to bring reconciliation. It will only be as the people of God put down roots that we may begin to see a change in our cities and our nation for Jesus' sake. It will only be as people of God step out of the safe haven of the fortress and begin to get involved in what's happening in our neighborhoods that we will begin to see transformation.

Arthur Matthews in his book "Ready for Battle" tells of the time he was under house arrest in China when he needed to have a reorientation of his spiritual compass, as the stress and pressures of his arrest heightened his desire to escape. Everything he saw passing his window suggested escape, from the swallows heading south to a little stick floating down the creek. They all pointed to a land beyond where he could escape and find freedom.

Even his Bible reading ran through the same filter so that everything seemed to point to escape, to the extent that he could build a strong case for it being the will of God, yet as he says, it was a distorted reading, because he had allowed his fears to control his desires and thus influence his mind-set.

"Once my compass was freed to respond to the Lord's mind,
I could easily see how my fears and desires had been blinding
me to the obvious. Surely, since God had put me in Communist
China, he must intend me to stay there

for his purpose until his time was fulfilled.
I have never forgotten that lesson in spiritual navigation." [1.]

The Missionary Call Came with Freedom:

When word came to the exiles to "build houses and settle down" they were being told they were going to have freedom where they were, freedom to move about and establish themselves. Though they were in exile they were not slaves and essentially, they were being told therefore not to act like they were. There was a liberty of movement and life.

Psalm 137 indicates for us however that at least initially the exiles didn't understand this message. Their lament was "How can we sing the Lord's song in a strange land?" They had adopted an attitude of self-pity that would so enslave them as to disable them. Would we not consider it a door opening if one of our neighbors or co-workers came up to one day and said, "Hey! Would you sing for me one of your worship songs I've been hearing about.?"

But the exiles could not see themselves doing it away from the Temple in Jerusalem. For them when it came to singing the great songs of joyful testimony relating the mighty, saving acts of Jehovah the Babylonians were not the preferred audience.

How tragic it is that then and even now when we prefer the slavery we know to the freedom we don't know! In the Church we become slaves to our routines, methodology, or programs or even worse when we move from the grace that sets people free to new forms of legalism as we relate to each other or other congregations. They don't baptize the way we do, they don't pray like we do, they don't worship like we do, they don't live like we do, etc. They all become statements of separation as we elevate our ways and denigrate one another's.

Pharisaic expressions are not restricted to the first century. As a young Christian steeped in the Reformed tradition, I remember hearing regularly that were serious doubts about the salvation of anyone who wasn't Reformed. I learned quickly that there were lots of people who loved Jesus and wanted to reach the lost with whom there would be great distances in theology, but they were just as much my brothers and sisters in Christ and in serving the Great Commission and the Great Commandment as anyone in my little Reformed world.

Even more tragic is the slavery we choose for our lives, whether it be to addictions with substance abuse, behaviorally, in attitudes of control, perfectionism, and abuse, or even the tendency many have to hold on to old wounds and re-live bad experiences by perpetuating them in others. It's true, hurting people hurt people. The amounts of pain, unresolved conflicts or wounds, and other assorted garbage many people are prepared to carry in their lives, rather than seek the healing available, is testimony to the degree to which we are prepared to let our lives be enslaved. There is a freedom that could be ours beginning internally that can never be taken away.

God's word through Jeremiah to the exiles was to use the freedom they had to build houses and settle down. Is this not a call to get established, to get to know our neighbors and get involved in our communities? The missionary call comes with the freedom to be ourselves but also to tell our story; to not be ashamed of being Christian but to 'sing the Lord's song' to those who ask to hear. The day in which we live places high value on the telling of "our" personal story. Though the age may be relativistic and the culture's interpretation of truth subjective, there is a willingness to hear what "works" by way of personal testimony from credible witnesses, people we know, not TV stooges shilling their products.

Charles Simeon (1759-1836) was a theological student at King's College, Cambridge in England at a time when Cambridge was not the scenic university town but a community in chaos. Impoverished rural people were pouring into town from the countryside to feed the Industrial Revolution, living in crumbling hovels in the back streets, poor and dirty. With them came a clash of worlds. The well-to-do Cambridge residents and students saw these peasants as a blight on their community and couldn't stand the thought of sharing "space' with them. Perhaps typical of the attitude was the historic 700-year-old Holy Trinity Church, once Catholic, then Anglican and now reduced to a handful of congregants, most of whom could care less about the fate of the poor around them. Simeon stood at one time outside this church praying: "Lord give me this church so that I may minister to these people."

Simeon was made vicar by the Bishop not because of his gifts or abilities but because no one else was interested. He began his ministry by going door to door throughout the parish with a simple introduction and request: 'My name is Simeon. I have called to enquire if I can do anything for your welfare." The poor peasants were attracted by his friendliness and began to attend Holy Trinity which created an unholy stir. Because of the unwashed, stench of their clothes the peasants often offended the other richer members who had paid rents for their pews and were now appalled at the sort of company they were being forced to keep. Predictably, they protested to the bishop to get rid of their minister who was the instigator of all the trouble, but the bishop retained Simeon saying that a little life was better than death.

The bishop's non-cooperation escalated the problem such that the wealthy members boycotted the morning services, locked their pews so that they were inaccessible, and hired a guest lecturer to preach to them on Sunday afternoons, away from the rancid poor and more in the manner to which they were accustomed. Simeon, not to be undone, out of his forty-nine pound a year salary, bought lumber and made portable benches for his Sunday morning congregation, which he placed in the aisles and foyer each Sunday before opening the doors to the poor of the city, a practice which he maintained for eleven years thinking, "If half the people get a double blessing, I'll be satisfied."

In the twelfth year revival fell and with it the wall of conflict came down. Simeon stayed another 54 years continuing his work with the poor. He was made dean of the theological faculty at king's College five times and influenced dozens of young pastors. Out of his ministry God raised up InterVarsity Christian Fellowship, the Cambridge Seven, a mission to China, C.T. Studd and Henry Martyn who went to India and translated the Bible into Urdu. During this whole time he would travel monthly to London to meet William Wilberforce, Lord Shaftsbury and others, with a view to abolishing slavery. (2.) Charles Simeon took the freedom that went with his missionary call, put down roots and influenced not just a community but more than a generation of people.

If the Church will hear the voice of God speaking to her today, she must hear the missionary call to bless the city, the communities where we are located, big or small, to buy our lumber and build benches where people can meet God through Jesus Christ. Surely putting down roots is about being a blessing where God has called us to be today, blessing our families, our workplace, our neighborhoods, and our communities. Surely it's about being the kind of people other people, especially including non-believes want to be around because they see in us something different, something which whets their appetite to *"taste and see that the Lord is good."*

> Proverbs 11:10-11 *"When the righteous prosper, the city rejoices; when the wicked perish, there are shouts of joy. Through the blessing of the upright a city is exalted...."*

The Missionary Call Came When The Harvest Was Ripe.

As Judah found itself in Babylon it was being called to refocus. There was a basic conflict of vision that had blinded Judah and before it, Israel; a conflict related to where God fit in their lives, if He did at all. Their present predicament was a symptom of their past unfaithfulness to God. Their blindness caused them to not only replace God's priorities with their own but also to replace God with their deities du jour, resulting in their present "Woe is me!" As they sat by the waters of Babylon they wept for past glory and comfort, feeling sorry for themselves, unable to see the opportunity being presented to them. God was calling them to take their eyes off themselves long enough to see a larger picture. He had brought them to where they were and had a plan for them.

In Psalm 137:1-4 we hear their lament:

"By the rivers of Babylon, we sat down and wept when we remembered Zion. There on the poplars we hung our harps, for there our captors asked us for songs, our tormentors demanded songs of joy; they said, 'Sing us the songs of Zion!' How can we sing the songs of the Lord while in a foreign land?"

Judah was feeling sorry for herself. In the minds of the exiles singing the songs of Zion was incompatible with their experience. How could they sing the Lord's song when the symbol of His presence, and therefore the substance, was far removed from them by these barbarians who had carried them off? Yet the people to whom they had been brought were asking questions, providing opportunities they were not prepared to see.

The Psalmist tells us that their captors asked them to sing. Now it may have been in mockery that they proposed such a thing but suppose for a moment that it is actually a matter of curiosity, having heard about the "Songs of Zion" and the reputation of singing these people had. Clearly, some knowledge of Judah and her people had preceded her. Then the question becomes one not of derision but of openness, of interest to hear about "your God." Might it be that it is evidence God has already been at work preparing the Babylonians for His missionaries? Possibly, in saying 'build houses and settle down" God was saying, "See the opportunity and seize it."

When my wife and I lived in Northern Ontario a popular place for cross-country skiing was at the nearby Provincial Park. On Saturdays and Sundays people would flock there for the groomed trails and the wander through the park. Since my day off was Monday, we often had the park to ourselves. Because we were novice skiers however, we found that we spent most of our time watching the trail in our attempt to keep the skis in the tracks and avoid the tumbles into trees and snowbanks that would otherwise inevitably follow.

We suspected, however, that there was more to view in the park than what we were seeing. So, on the advice of a friend, we took up snowshoeing, enabling us to walk naturally without having to focus on the placement of our feet. The result was the park came alive. We began to see all kinds of birds, animals, and tracks that we had never seen before, and would not have seen with our eyes glued to the groomed ski trail.

Sometimes as Christians and as the Church we lose focus. We get so caught up in the host of noble things we do that we sometimes forget what priority our relationship to God is and what our primary purpose is. Our vision gets blurry at times when it comes to remembering that Jesus Christ is the head of our church, not tradition, money, nor politics and that our mandate is as to be missionaries to our world.

We sometimes assume that anyone who doesn't go to church isn't interested or we assume that sharing our faith will be interpreted wrongly and we'll lose friends, so we say nothing. We busy ourselves with our family and church tracks and become blind to the "life' around us.

The exiles needed to see that maybe there was a ripening happening in Babylon and that they were to be the ones to gather in the harvest. The harvest could not be gathered by those who were running away or preoccupied with themselves, it could only be gathered by people who in compassion and grace could see the opportunity and seize it. People all around us today are open like they have not been in a long time. The shattering of the illusion of the innate goodness and potential of modern man, the disappointment with things institutional which have failed or been scandalized, and a host of other factors have given breed to a time in which people are hungry for something bigger and more transcendent than human life. People are hungry but hungry people are not always discerning about what they eat and herein lies the opportunity for the Church in exile today to come forward with the offer of the heavenly manna, Jesus Christ, and tell our story.

There is an open door being presented to the Church today for credible witnesses to go through, but you can't be a credible witness to a Muslim with a beer in your hands, you can't speak to a Hindu of holy days as you cut your grass on Sunday, your holy day, and you can't witness to Joe Canadian about how much your life has changed when it looks just the same as everybody else's in the culture and has espoused the values of the world rather than the standards of God.

This is not the day for Christians to relax and enjoy the creature comforts gained while we pat ourselves on the back about the level of enlightenment we have attained compared to the militant legalism of our forefathers. It is not a day where we can simply ask if something is right or wrong to determine the standard for Christian living but must also ask if our actions lend or destroy credibility for Jesus. Whether we have grown in grace to such an extent that we can do things others in the Kingdom cannot is not the question; (Is it right for Christians to drink alcohol, smoke, go to bars and clubs, live together outside of marriage, etc.?) The crucial question which goes beyond the right and wrong, is whether the activity we are engaging in conveys the right message about us as Christians and about the gospel. The tendency in recent years in terms of lifestyle has been to so broaden the grace available as to obliterate any lines of distinction between Christian and non-Christian. Our move to culture's periphery began when those lines got more and more blurry.

There is a crisis today not just for our cities but in our churches. The crisis for our cities has to do with what kind of communities will exist in the future and the crisis for our churches is whether we will be credible witnesses or forever in exile on the periphery of life. God's call is to put in the sickle where we are, to gather the harvest, be committed to our communities and to be a blessing within them. Credibility comes from a record of integrity seen in faithfulness to our mission, consistency in character, and grace in its extension. It is time for the Church to awaken to its holy calling, to build houses and settle down, put down roots and bless the community. We don't have the option of saying: "It's too dirty! It's too smelly! It's too much work!" It is our community. Larry Crabb in his book *Becoming A True Christian Community*, suggests that a good way to understand spiritual community is that it is one where it is "a safe place to hit bottom." He talks about the power of authentic Christian community and suggests there are four statements that occur in authentic Christian community we all need to experience:

1. **I SEE YOU**: warts and all, your baser passions which I don't like but I will not turn away from you.

2. **I ACCEPT YOU**; as you are with all your brokenness and problems

3. **I BELIEVE IN YOU**: more particularly, I believe in what you can become in Christ.

4. **I POUR INTO YOU:** I see what's wonderful within you and I am willing to invest in you and your future.

ENDNOTES

1. Arthur Matthews: Ready for Battle, pg. 19-20

2. Raye Bakke: The Urban Christian, pg.19-20

3. Larry Crabb: Becoming A True Spiritual Community, pg. 142

CHAPTER FOUR

REDISCOVERING FRUITFULNESS

Jeremiah 29:5
"...plant gardens and eat what they produce."

A single, middle aged man one day decided he would go on a Caribbean cruise. On the first day of the voyage as he was walking on the deck an attractive woman about his age passed by smiling at him in a friendly manner as she did so. He not only took note of her smile and delighted in her friendliness, but he also made arrangements that evening to be seated at the same table as the woman for dinner. As conversation developed, he commented on having seen her earlier in the day and expressed how warmed he had been by her friendly smile. When she heard this, she smiled and said, "Well the reason I smiled was because when I saw you I was immediately struck by your strong resemblance to my second husband." At this the man's heart shrank, his ears perked up and he asked "Oh, how many times have you been married?" She gazed at him with a bashful, Princess Diana look and as she smiled she answered, "Once." I suspect she was not only creative but very productive when it came to getting results.

Jeremiah calls the exiles to switch gears and join the ranks of the creative and productive in his next step.

Mission Strategy for Today's Church:
Step 2 - Be Productive Factors.

As we have seen the first missionary strategy is to put down roots. We recognize that missionary call of God came to them with an open time frame. They wanted to believe they were going back home soon but they were being called to be productive influences in Babylon a long time, 70 years. To that end, they were to hear that missionary call as one which came with freedom. They were in exile, but they could do most of the things they had normally done except they would do them in Babylon instead of Jerusalem or Judah.

As a missionary call it came to them when the time was right, when the harvest was ripe. Babylon was asking questions of the people of Judah. They wanted to hear "the Lord's Song." This missionary call we have seen is summarized in the commitment required to put down roots and bless the community where we live.

Jeremiah now gives us the second strategy, to be productive factors in our communities. If we recognize that one of the effective missionary strategies available is to put down roots, to make a commitment to a neighborhood, or a community, then we also have to hear the word that Jeremiah gives to the people of Judah in their exile when he says to them "plant gardens and eat what they produce." It seems to me that Jeremiah is calling Judah to be productive where they were, to be productive factors in their community. In other words, don't sit there heaping ashes on yourself. Don't sit there feeling sorry for yourself. Don't sit there waiting for somebody else to hand you the solution to your problems. Do something about it. Be a productive factor in your community.

We need to recognize here that this word given through Jeremiah was earth shaking in terms of the unparalleled advice it was to the Hebrew people. Never before had they heard such a word. Their focus had always been previously getting back to the promised land, and yet to their credit, as history shows, over the centuries of dispersion Jews have followed this strategy given through Jeremiah. God was calling the people of Judah to be productive in their communities, to not only take care of themselves, but to resume normal living. Planting gardens and eating what they produce was not something you did if you were planning to take off the following week. It was something that required time and effort, something which was often communal in nature, in the planting, nurturing, harvesting, and celebrating. To plant a garden was to be productive people wherever they were placed.

This is precisely the call for the people of God today. To put down roots. To unpack our suitcases. To be productive factors in our cities. Judah in Babylon was not to act like they were slaves or prisoners. They were to conduct normal life and living. They were free to do so. They had the freedom to plant, the freedom to harvest. They had the freedom to eat from the labor of their own hands. Jeremiah here is putting great stock in a good work ethic, something that is highly valued in the scriptures.

> *Proverbs 10:4 "lazy hands make a man poor."*
> *Ecclesiastes 10:18 "if a man is lazy, the rafters sag."*
> *Hebrews 6:12 "we do not want you to become lazy."*

To be productive factors within the community a high priority is given to being industrious, to not sitting back waiting to receive whatever provisions were made for them by the Babylonians. They were to plant seed, provide for their own needs, be diligent, and active.

There are concerns involved here. One is that you not become a burden upon your community. And let's clarify this so that no false inferences can be made. There are times in the lives of people when we need to ask for help, when our resources become depleted. It may be because of losing our jobs, or through death, illness, divorce, or a whole host of reasons but where drastic changes in our situation mean that we no longer have the physical or emotional resources to provide for ourselves. At that point it is a privilege for the community to do so. Whether we're talking about the community of faith, the church, or whether we're talking about the geopolitical community as a whole, it is a privilege for the community of faith then to provide for the needs of those who have found themselves in such straights.

It is also possible, however, for another scene to play out. If we are in a situation where we have no resources, if everything is depleted from us because we've been lazy, or squandered what we have had, or because we have adopted the attitude that we don't have to do anything, that everything is owed us then that is a significant difference. If we refuse to take responsibility, for ourselves, if we've not taken the initiative to pursue a good work ethic then we should not expect the silver platter handed to us. The burden on a community is the attitude which refuses responsibility.

The work ethic that Jeremiah is highlighting is to be a people who are productive. Sometimes circumstances arise where you don't have the resources anymore, or where you feel diminished, but God can still use us even in those situations. It can also allow you to experience the benefits of your community, made up of people who have committed themselves to being productive, who can care for you and see it as a privilege to do so. Our African brothers and sisters can teach us so much about community in this regard.

The concern here is to be aware of the welfare of those around you and ready to assist. In the culture in which we live there's a very different rule of thumb that often is at work. It's the rule of thumb of taking care of yourself and basically forgetting about everybody else. Thank God for people who are trying to show that there is a better way of living. It's a way of caring for other people, of looking out for the welfare of not only yourself but of your friends, your neighbors, your family, of looking out for the welfare of your city and your nation.

Being free for the exiles meant they had the liberty to provide for themselves; to take their talents, their expertise and to put them to use. One of the things that we understand about the group of people who went into exile is that they were the cream of the crop. All the royal household went into exile, but there's an addendum that goes on the end of it that reminds us about some other people that were involved in the exile. In verse two we're told about people of the royal household who were taken and then at the tail end of the verse we also discover that the best craftsmen, and artisans were also taken. One of the concerns obviously was that Nebuchadnezzar was going to take advantage of the artisans and craftsmen and put them to work for himself, but what it says is that all the educated people, all the people with the talents and gifts were there in Babylon and could make a difference by their contribution. They could see their contribution as being forced because of captivity or they could see it as an opportunity to represent their God.

The story of Daniel relates how he took his talents and put them to work in captivity, becoming a success story in terms of how he applied his faith to the culture in which he found himself and how he maintained integrity of faith.

The word from Jeremiah is to be a productive factor. To be a productive factor in our community goes back to the first mission strategy. Being committed to the community. But it also means knowing your community and who lives in it, what characterizes it, where people work, what they do for a living.

In global tentmaker missions today, access is gained for Christians into restricted nations through free enterprise. The opportunity still exists for people to go into restricted access countries to set up businesses and employ people even with government support. The business provides a platform for not only making a productive contribution to that community, but also for the gospel to be shared. In Africa Inland Mission we have Christian teachers who are invited to teach in Islamic schools because of the quality education they bring and knowing they are believers in Jesus.

Perhaps the same opportunity is presenting itself here, whereby Christian businesspeople see their businesses as extensions of the local church mission or as investors in businesses which can open doors for people to find Christ. Are there opportunities for teachers, doctors, nurses, politicians, daycare workers to influence lives in our culture, even if it is only one life at a time? I think the answer is a definite "YES!"

Those who study cities have determined six categories in which you can list the various cities of the world. (1.) The first category is that of the cultural city which produces fashion, trends, and ideas. Places like San Francisco and Paris are cultural cities. Another type of city is the political or administrative city. It produces power and decisions. Cities like Ottawa, Washington, London and New Deli fit into this category of city. Another type of city is the industrial city, one which produces goods, like Chicago. Another type of city is the commercial city. It produces giant markets such as in New York. Another type of city is a symbolic city. It symbolizes either the division within the city or the nation, or the warfare, even the religious hatred that's involved in that area. Cities like Jerusalem, symbolize the inner struggles and turmoil resident there. The sixth category of cities is called the primary city. A primary city is a city that has all five of the other elements of the city involved in it. Cities like Berlin and Paris are called primary cities.

If we understand something about the city in which we live, we need also to understand something about the people who live in the cities. Relational networks are usually divided four ways - the biological network, the geographical network, the vocational network, and the recreational network. In the biological network are all the people to whom you are related - your family. With urbanization biological networks are often scattered. The vocational network has to do with all the people with whom you work. The geographical network has to do with the area from which you come, and the recreational network has to do with the people you come in contact with whether it's in your leisure, at your health club, the ball field, the hockey rink or wherever you take your leisure. In Canada, for eight months of the year the hockey rink is really the new temple.

One of the things that's important is the identity of urban dwellers. If you ask an urban dweller who they are they will usually describe themselves on the basis of what they do. If you ask a rural person who they are, they will typically describe themselves not on the basis of what they do but of either the family history or the geography in which they live. Suppose I ask a someone in Toronto who he is. Nine times out of ten he'll probably describe what he does. He will probably state that he is a teacher, in advertising, an accountant, etc. according to his vocation.

On the other hand if I am standing on the sidelines watching my daughter play soccer and meet someone there, chances are he or she will introduce himself/herself as a family member of one of the players and then describe his or her vocation. If I was to go out into rural Ontario, or more particularly if you went out into the Maritimes and into the west and you ask someone who they are, they will describe themselves based on their family network or where they live. I'm a Cape Bretoner, I'm a Newfoundlander, I'm from the Prairies. Where I grew up, the first question you ask after hearing a person's name is, "What's your father's name?" to make genealogical connection.

This is an important issue because if we recognize that urban dwellers take their identity from what they do then we begin to understand why unemployment is more than an economic issue. It's an issue of identity. When people lose their jobs in the city they often feel a loss of their identity, their sense of meaning, purpose, and significance. "No job" often translates into "no life".

If we understand these factors than we begin to understand something about the people with whom we live. We understand that the people in urban centres hunger for high quality and lasting fellowship. In a lot of cases, it's because they've left families behind to go and be involved in the workplace. As a consequence, where the church isn't developing relationships, building community, then you find places like the health clubs, the neighborhood pubs become the local dispensers of friendship, fellowship and therapy, and I don't need to tell you the danger of amateur therapy dispensed in the neighborhood pub.

Urban people protect themselves from casual, superficial relationships as well, recognizing that urban life is mobile. The people you develop friendships with may be here today and in Singapore tomorrow. Urban people put up walls and they try to protect themselves in a few "safe" relationships. One of the realities of today is that we are psychologically overloaded and overstimulated by the constant and immediate messages delivered by media to all our devices. People in cities suffer psychological overload from the pressures of work, of family, of leisure, the pressures of being bombarded constantly by sales messages everywhere they go, the bombardment of graphic news and entertainment that is readily available and with the noise, the sheer numbers of people they rub elbows with on the subway, the bus, or sitting in traffic and the speed of life in the city.

I used to tell people when I moved from Sydney to Halifax my pace picked up by five steps and when I moved from Halifax to Toronto my pace picked up by ten. It tells you something about the exhilarated speed of life in the city. We want what we want, and we want it now. We're not prepared to wait. Everything comes at a faster pace in the city, and with it there are thousands of casual relationships people are involved in each day. If you take public transit to work, you encounter hundreds if not thousands of people every day. One of the reasons why people don't talk to each other on the subways and on the buses is because of the relational anxiety and wanting to keep themselves from being extended too far. The more people you know, the more stories from them you carry, and the more you are expected to care. People filter out what they can't deal with and in many cases they become numb to the events in the cities around them.

When Kitty Genevisie was murdered in New York she cried out in the streets of her own neighborhood for twenty minutes while her neighbors looked out of their apartment and house windows and watched her death. (2.)

Psychologists and criminologists who looked at that event in New York City asked the question, what happened to our community? Why did no one come to her aid? Their conclusion was no one helped because of the psychological overload that so many people deal with where they either block out the things they don't want to deal with or can't deal with. Some people survive by not thinking about what they do or what they see. We become blind and deaf to the sights and sounds of life around us, preoccupied with our own self-preservation.

I can't help but think about medical researchers who are doing the research for tobacco companies. If ever there was a case for skewed research it must be the medical research funded by the tobacco companies with the hope their studies will come to the conclusion that it's okay to smoke, when all other evidence points to the health hazards. Some people see what they want to see and hear what they want to hear. It's a fact of life in the city that we need to recognize.

We need to recognize that relationships are being withdrawn not extended in the city. A Sony spokesman spoke about the power of a Sony Walkman. In the crowded public transit system of Japan Sony determined they could carve out an individual environment for each person by allowing individuals to own portable cassette/CD players with earphones, which could be plugged into whatever your listening desire is while unplugging yourself from the world around you. You can be standing elbow to elbow in the subway and as far as Sony is concerned you have created for yourself your own world, your own environment. Yet the Walkman is nothing compared to what is available on our phones today and with our noise cancelling earphones connected we send a clear signal, "I'm not available to you!" That's a picture in many ways of the life in the city where we isolate ourselves, we cocoon.

BUT God is bringing the world to our doorsteps. What will be our mission strategy be as the world arrives next door? Will we abandon our neighborhoods? Will we be committed to our neighborhoods? Will we put down roots? Will we seek to be productive factors in our communities?

It seems that the mission strategy God gave Jeremiah for the exiles in Judah works and has always worked. Maybe we need to rediscover it today; being committed our neighborhoods, putting down roots, becoming productive factors where God has placed us. God invites us to use the talents has given us, to plant gardens and eat what they produce.

The exiles in Babylon could discover the great opportunity God was handing them only when they changed their attitude towards their circumstances and their captors, determining instead to make their situation work. "Planting gardens and eating what they produce" would not just be a way of enduring the trial but of learning obedience and therefore the blessings that go with it.

Henry Blackaby in his book "Experiencing God" writes about finding out where God is working and then joining Him in what he is doing as the right attitude for the believer. You may recall that it was actually Jesus' attitude. (John 5:19) Judah would discover that God was already working in the lives of the people of Babylon. The question they would have to answer for themselves was whether they would join Him. Blackaby lists seven realities of experiencing

God which Judah needed to discover and which we may need to discover for our cities today:

1. God is always at work around you.
2. God pursues a continuing love relationship with you that is real and personal.

3. God invites you to become involved with Him in His work.
4. God speaks by the Holy Spirit through the Bible, prayer, circumstances, and the Church to reveal Himself, His purposes, and His ways.
5. God's invitation for you to work with Him always leads you to a crisis of belief that requires faith and action.
6. You must make major adjustments in your life to join God in what He is doing.
7. You come to know God by experience as you obey Him and He accomplishes His work through you. (3.)

Judah confused its experience of religion for an experience of God which translated into exile. To now experience God, it would require a crisis of faith, major adjustments in their lives, and full obedience. The same may be true of the Church today. The cultural landscape has changed all around us and now as strangers in our own land we find ourselves working with different definitions of productivity, many of which have more to do with creative genius than divine inspiration. If the local congregation will be productive, we must rediscover prayer, as the powerhouse behind all ministry but even more importantly that it is in prayer where God opens our eyes to see where He is working, inviting us to pick up our rakes and shovels.

It amazes me that we can fill auditoriums today with church leaders who will pay to hear the latest "How To...." seminars but it is near impossible to get those same leaders together to pray for their city. What's wrong with that picture? We read tremendous stories of people like Jim Cymbala [4.] and how a church built on prayer has been a productive influence on its city. Yet our response is not to get on our knees to seek the heart of God for our community but to attempt to duplicate programs instead.

God is at work in our cities. He is gathering the nations into them where people are more willing to hear credible testimonies of faith that works than ever before. According to the Joshua Project there are 296 people groups in Canada, 62 or almost 21% of whom are in unreached people groups.[5.] Canada expects to see 500,000 new immigrants by 2025 but as we've seen they haven't provided infrastructure for them and many are living on the street. So many of those who come are from creative access nations where they are restricted from hearing the Gospel, but away from those restrictions in Canada are open to hearing from credible witnesses. Is there an opportunity for the followers of Jesus to make a difference?

The beauty of this season is the power given to personal story, and we have the greatest story ever to be heard. It requires a medium that is credible however, "produced" from obedience, and able to say, "It works!" People from other religious backgrounds will listen to credible witnesses. Churches involved in making their communities better and safer places to live, involved in changing people's lives, socially, economically, emotionally, and spiritually are the ones who are "planting gardens and eating what they produce."

ENDNOTES

1. Ray Bakke - The Urban Christian, pgs. 37-41

2. Ray Bakke - The Urban Christian, pgs, 41-42

3. Henry Blackaby with Claude V. King - Experiencing God, pg. 50

4. Jim Cymbala - Fresh Faith

5.   The Joshua Project - https://joshuaproject.net/countries/CA

CHAPTER 5

BRINGING STABILITY

Jeremiah 29:6a
"Marry and have sons and daughters. Find wives for your sons and give your daughters in marriage, so that they too have sons and daughters. Increase in number there;
do not decrease."

A parent/teacher council was held one day to consider the serious matter of after school programs. After several suggestions were received such as building new playgrounds, developing bicycle trails, drop-in centres, computer labs, and basketball programs, one grandmother finally chirped in with, "Why don't they just go home?"

Though the solution seems simple it is only simple if home has someone there to care for you. Unfortunately, that is not the case for many children today. In Ontario the government has talked about legislating teacher participation in after-school programs, partly because there is a need for them and partly because alternate resources are not available.

When God, through Jeremiah, gave the above instructions to Judah He was saying: "Be a stabilizing influence in your community." Marrying and having both children and grandchildren is a comment on the commitment of families to both stay and influence what happens around them. If the exiles were not going to unpack their suitcases and stay, they would certainly not think about settling down, having children, and raising a generation or two of people walking in a faith relationship to God. So, an attitude adjustment was required. If Judah recognized that God had brought them to Babylon for a purpose, and that they were going to be there for a while (29:4-5) then they might begin to think in terms of settling down to make the best of it. They were not only to stabilize their own lives but through their influence and numbers they were to be a stabilizing force in the community.

The one thing that can deliver the maximum amount of stability to any given community, city, or culture is a stable family and home. It is God's building block for communities and society. When the family undergoes brokenness, the culture follows. When the family unit is healthy and whole, community and culture follow. When the family is de-stabilized so follows society. In 1994 according to the polls, 63% of Canadians believe the family was in crisis. [1.] While many believe that the divorce rate in the country is increasing it is actually stable at worst. How much of that stability is because fewer people are both getting divorced and married is unknown. Divorce however is not the only factor which creates the impression of crisis.

Two income families with children increasingly feel the stress fractures of trying to maintain busy careers, homes, and families. According to Rec Media this is what the Canadian family looks like today:

67% are married
16% are single parents
17% are common law
There are 464,335 blended families

17% of couples in Canada have no religious affiliation. One in five Canadians were born outside of the country. [2.]

A sidebar linking income level to family status would show that families with two parents are most well off. Single parent dads with children are next best off, and single parent moms were more often than not, living under the poverty line. All of this begs the question: "What happens when things go wrong in the family?"

One of the factors to be acknowledged as contributing to stress in the home is what is called "Second Shift." Over 67% of all Canadian women are employed full time, and yet as they have moved into the workplace men have not taken a proportionate responsibility for housework and childcare. [3.] Women in the workplace work a full day and then come home to begin the "second shift" of a full evening caring for their families. Studies have shown that employed women more often consider the option of divorce than those at home.

A second factor in why things go wrong in our families is poor communication. We bring with us into our marriages what was normal in our family of origin. If our birth family was dysfunctional in any way it, as often as not, becomes our normal. Healthy patterns of communication fall into this category. According to research done by Regina Divorce Lawyer among all the factors that lead people to consider divorce the breakdown in communication seems to feed into all of them. [4.] There are a number of factors which go into the desire for better communication in our homes, not the least of which are our busy schedules. In two income families it is especially hard to maintain upward career momentum, let alone a high standard of work usually equated with long hours, and still maintain a balanced home life.

Increasingly Canadian families are dependent on someone outside the family to provide care through the workday for their children. In might be a family member, a friend, a paid provider but the balancing of work and family has become a real juggling act.

Every time there is a school strike we hear the cries for help and during COVID we saw it all accentuated when one parent had to either give up their jobs or find ways to work from home and care for their children. According to Statistics Canada in 2022 52% of Canadian women are providing care for children and care-dependent adults, compared to 42% of men. 31% of Canadians cared for children under 15 years of age. Of that number 28% are unpaid, 1% are a combination of paid and unpaid, 2% are paid, and 69% have no care. Of those unpaid caregivers more than half expressed being worried or anxious, women more than the men. 48% of men expressed being tired compared to 62% of women, and 37% of men expressed being worried while 50% of women did. When it comes to feeling overwhelmed 27% of men say they are compared 45% of women. [5.]

Canadians are struggling to keep it together. The reality is that the busier we are the harder it is to get time together, let alone time for healthy communication. Communication requires time that is both quality and in quantity, and energy that is more than leftovers from a busy day. Spouses and children get the leftovers of our time and energy too often, after we have made more bricks with less straw for our masters. The upswing in mental health issues today in our workplaces, schools, and homes is moving towards a crisis unless something changes.

Since COVID many workers have been working from home and a recent social survey by Statistics Canada shows that 70% of those working from home all the time are more satisfied with the amount of time they spend with family while 60% of those working outside of the home were more satisfied. For workers with children, working from home all the time 67% reported high satisfaction with the amount of time spent with family, compared to 56% of those working outside the home. [6.]

A further reality in our homes is that the values once instilled and reinforced at home by parents is being replaced by the values of either the culture at large or by the state. Our children in school are being bombarded by cultural and state values that may not reflect the values of the home but where dissent increasingly is not tolerated. Unfortunately, we also find that the care provided by outsiders has great potential for abuse. One of the results is that we find increasingly is fractured, broken lives hungry for wholeness. I was amazed at the Urbana Missionary Conference in years ago at the attention given to issues of brokenness and abuse. What I discovered in talking to InterVarsity staff was that these were the most frequent issues they faced on their campuses and that it was imperative to deal with them at this stage before these students would go out on either a short or long-term mission and have them explode there.

The increased complexity of relationships both at home and beyond makes it difficult for young people to arrive on the university campus whole. Today's young people are fluent in the language of brokenness and can admit to being broken people, but it seems to be more of a generic admission than an actual ownership of the details of our brokenness.

Related to busy schedules impacting communication is the apparent diminishing of communication skills many have. Many people do not know how to adequately communicate. They do not recognize that communication involves both speaking and listening, and further do not seem to understand that how we deliver our communication is as important as the content, both in tone and posture. Many are either ignorant or just uncaring about the how the power of words and tones can destroy life or inspire it. When we do not have good communication the temptation to throw away time becomes all but irresistible.

So, what is the point of all this statistical mumbo jumbo? Simply this, life in the Canadian family has become increasingly complex with forces at work we have never had to deal with before. One statistical surveyor suggested that Canadian parents should essentially get a medal for bravery as they are the first generation to have children pretty much born with the screen in their hands. There are outside influences today that exert enormous pressure on our children and our homes to conform to the values of the day, whether they are examined values and healthy or not. The family unit which once formed the foundation for our society is being shaped by TV, the local day care, or our schools. Children and spouses, once a priority in the home play second and third fiddle to career and leisure, and the training of our children is left to professionals with cultural values increasingly dictated by the state..

It may seem obvious to say that it is best for our children if we can keep Mom and Dad together in a whole relationship but unfortunately it seems increasingly difficult to do it. Tragically, things happen and brokenness results for all parties. Christ, however, can put the broken pieces of our lives together allowing us to be whole, functional people. The same Christ sends us to the broken people and families of our communities to minister hope and healing in His name. It here that the church has an opportunity today to model healthy relationships and values for our communities.

When God spoke through Jeremiah concerning the family, He invited the exiles to commit to a healthy, whole model for living which would not only benefit themselves but the larger community as well. Similarly, the Christian family, rediscovered as a foundation block for our communities, can have a stabilizing effect on culture at large through the quiet testimony of winsome, whole lives dedicated to selfless rather than selfish living, to values based on something that lasts rather than the accumulation of 'things"; through dedication to the betterment of the individuals and community through the gospel of Jesus Christ.

What is the hope for our cities? It is in people committed to the most stabilizing unit of society - the family, where we learn to partner together to bring the best out of each other, where we learn to communicate better, where we encourage one another, bear each other in weakness, and lovingly correct when we wander. In so doing we can model a better way for living in community together. God's strategy for the exiles was to influence their world by the stability of their homes, their everyday lives, lived out in faith, and by their sheer numbers through their children, the marrying of their children, and their grandchildren, all walking in a real faith. God said: "Increase in number there; do not decrease."

The exiles could not let the despair about the circumstances cause them to wither and decrease. Instead, they were to be life-giving, life-sustaining, and life inspiring. Imagine the Babylonian response to their captives who treated their captors like they had just done them the greatest favor in the world and who were so full of life and hope that it was hard not to be infected with the contagion of their faith. Having children and grandchildren gives us the opportunity to pass along our values based on our life-giving relationship to God through Christ. As our children have children who have children these values spread but it begins in our homes right now.

The missionary call to Judah was to put down roots, be productive influences, and be stabilizing factors in the community. In Jeremiah's day this message was revolutionary. It is no less today. The same missionary call comes to the Church in exile today.

As Christians today we could have communities of hope, healing, and refuge to offer to the scattered and broken peoples of the world living on our doorsteps. The irony is not lost on me when I realize that instead of going to the mission field God has brought the mission field to me and to our community of faith. Through things like ESL, children's and youth programs, after school programs, employment counselling, etc. and the love of the Christian community we can help stabilize the chaos of resettlement and positively influence our community. The catch is that we will have to think more strategically and work more intentionally at reaching out rather than hiding within.

Having said this, it is not to minimize the need still for people who are willing to exercise the same kind of ministry by going the nations with the Gospel of Christ. In Africa alone there are over 900 unreached people groups who have never heard of Jesus. Many of those groups are open to listen and learn, if only someone would go. The harvest fields still wait for the laborers.

For communities divided by racism and prejudice the Christian community can model reconciliation, love, and acceptance of all people regardless of race, colour, etc. In Christ we offer the ultimate personal relationship for all people and all families; single-parent, double, or no parents at all and we offer the One who can bring stability into the most chaotic of lives and homes. In the last ten years we have seen how easily rhetoric can divide and polarize leading to the increase in hate and violence.

The Church, if it can learn more wholesome patterns of communication and relating, can assist struggling families, the couples and communities in crisis. The Christian community can be leaders in eliminating racism and hatred. The Christian community, worshipping and working together can offer the friendship and support needed to bring healing and wholeness to a host of people and surely that is what it means to be light and salt.

For years, before the master agreement was changed by the government, the church I pastored in Scarborough sponsored refugees seeking a new start, most of whom were "Boat People" fleeing Vietnam, but later a number came from places like Afghanistan as well. At last count we had sponsored something in the neighborhood of over 900 refugees. There is great delight in our congregation when occasionally one of these refugees returns to show us how well they are now doing. People who arrived with only the clothes on their backs now are productive members of our community and country, and we delight with them at the graduation from university of their children and the "success" of their lives.

The ministry of bringing and caring for these people over the years probably did more to breathe life into our congregation than any other single factor, not to mention what it did for those who came as refugees. It taxed and stretched us but it was good for us, like so much of what God invites us to do with Him.

Today there are opportunities abounding to make a difference. At one point in Scarborough our youth groups combined with groups from neighboring churches in an activity that made the TV news for going out and cleaning the watercourse and ravine beside our facility which is a catch basin for all kinds of garbage and contraband. It was such a simple idea but it said to the community that all the news you hear about youth violence is not all the news there is about youth. Here was a group trying to make a difference in the community.

The Church in exile still has solutions it can offer to our ailing communities, but we cannot rest on yesterday's accomplishments or methods. Our stabilizing strategies will grow out of the creative process of actually recognizing what the community and spiritual realities of this day and season are and then integrate faith and life in credible, tangible ways. Put down roots, be productive influences, and be stabilizing factors! Heed the missionary call! Our culture has traded the stability of real community for Facebook, TikTok, and a world of sound bytes with no real connection. It is time for the Church to be a real family again and offer life to our communities. God has placed us where we are purposefully to bring light and hope into a world that grows increasingly dark.

ENDNOTES

1. MacLean's Magazine - June 20th, 1994, pg. 31

2. https://recmedia.com/blog/the-modern-canadian-family/

3. https://www150.statcan.gc.ca/n1/pub/75-006-x/2022001/article/00009-eng.htm

4. https://reginadivorcelawyer.ca/top-10-reasons-for-divorce-in-canada/

5. https://www150.statcan.gc.ca/n1/pub/11-627-m/11-627-m2023004-eng.htm

6. https://www150.statcan.gc.ca/n1/daily-quotidien/220221/dq220221a-eng.htm

CHAPTER 6:

THE BLESSING OF THE STRANGERS

Jeremiah 29:7
"Also, seek the peace and prosperity of the city to which I have carried you into exile."

Douglas Walrath tells the story of a 76-year-old women who had lived all her life in the same community, attending the same church. When the building had last been refurbished 30 years previously, she donated the second stained glass window on the right wall in memory of her parents. Now the building was falling badly into disrepair with the ministry not far behind it. The pastor of the local Presbyterian congregation was essentially pastoring her United Methodist congregation as well, which was also suffering. Ultimately one building would be closed and one congregation formed. The thought of that closure had caused Mary, the elderly saint. to break down in tears saying "I don't think I can leave this building. I know all the practical reasons why we can't go on but I'm frightened. I don't know whether I will be able to pray in another building!" [1.]

In another community a young pastor came to a small rural parish and discovered that every Sunday morning at the stroke of twelve the stately grandfather clock at the front of the sanctuary tolled out all twelve bells essentially ending the service whether it was over or not. The pastor discovered that the clock had been donated by one of the leading families in the congregation as a memorial gift, making its significance well beyond the proportion of its size.

After some time, the young pastor grew weary of the clock's routine and decided to move it to the back of the building where it would be hopefully less intrusive in the service. Amazingly, when he came in on Sunday the clock was back in its place. The next week he moved it again only to have it back up front for Sunday, and on and on repeated the game until finally the clock was up front and the pastor was gone.

These stories tell us about real problems in the Church today and about our attachment to things like clocks, windows, traditions, or routines. Mary would eventually with the pastor's help find the grace and strength to make the transition to her new church but many handle the changes and transitions involved in either new facilities or new ways of ministering with much less grace, as evidenced in the old clock. We do well to realize how easy it is to begin to lean on many of the things around the church which supplant our leaning on the Everlasting Arms.

I used to show our church in Orleans a picture from the 60's of the main downtown street in Sydney, where I grew up. It was well defined and everyone new how to navigate the one-way streets and cross streets to get where you wanted to go. I suggested that it reflected the world of the church and more particularly the training I was given in seminary in preparation for ministry. It had well defined roles and expectations. Then I would show a logging road, roughly hewn through a forest and barely passable. I then suggested that it was a picture of ministry today. Nothing in seminary prepared me for the world we live in today and how much ministry has changed. Consider the steep learning curve many pastors and church leaders had to go through during Covid lockdowns to stream their services online in some form. It brought most into the 20th century, one step closer to the century in which we actually live. In some respects it would be nice to hang out with Mary in the old church, but God invites us to join Him in what he is doing in new ways today.

Judah in her captivity felt it was impossible to live, let alone worship, in the land and presence of the Babylonians. The message of Jeremiah simply cut the exiles adrift from everything they considered essential to their well-being and on which they had depended. The Temple which was the centre of religious and social life was in ruins and they were captives in a land far away not only geographically, but emotionally and spiritually as well. The political system they were accustomed to, the army, the kingship, their national borders were all gone; all the things in which they had seen the presence of the Lord were gone.

The mission God was calling them to embrace and become engaged in required of them major adjustments. The slide to captivity for Judah had happened so insidiously that before they knew it their whole relationship to God had changed, the substance of their faith was replaced by the forms of religion. We are reminded of Blackaby's principle, "You must make major adjustments in your life to join God in what He is doing." [2.]

Not unlike the exiles of Judah we get very confused about the difference between the substance of faith and the forms of faith, perhaps nowhere more so than in the word "church" itself. Church today by common usage refers to a place of worship or facility for ministry. Yet the biblical definition is that of a group of people (believers) gathered together around a common commitment to Jesus

Christ and His mission. It is a living organism, referred to as the Body of Christ.

As such it is not about place, not a static entity, but a living body; dynamic and mobile in the service of God, a people of tents not towers. We get wrapped up in buildings and programs often perpetuating yesterday rather than creating a tomorrow, with ministry revolving around servicing and satisfying the saints instead of reaching out and saving the sinners. Budgets get driven by maintaining a building while outreach and ministry die of neglect.

If when we enter a place of worship on Sunday and sing "O worship the King!" but find there is neither the majesty nor the presence of the King, but instead find a choir in tension, allegiance to forms and rituals, and people listening more for the ticking of the clock than for the Word of the Lord, then we might ask ourselves whether we have not also slipped from Jerusalem to Babylon. Often the prophetic nerve of pastors and Christian leaders has been severed for fear of upsetting the "saints", which might otherwise lead to a healthy engaging of our culture with the gospel.

Leonard Sweet in Soul Tsunami said this:

"More US Americans believe in God, in miracles, and in prayer than ever before. Yet more of us are in moral crisis than ever before. Radio talk-show host Dr. Laura Schlesinger asserted on NBC's Meet The Press that one of the reasons why is because of clergy. 'I yell at clergy all the time,' she admitted. 'I think the clergy - with all due respect - have become more like camp counsellors than leaders. What they are doing is saying, I want people to come back next week. You can't challenge them too much, can't ask too much, can't tell them that religion demands something of them. God demands something of you.'" [3.]

109

Sadly, in vast portions of the Church we want 15 minute sermons, one hour services, (less is even better) and nothing unusual to push our comfortabilities, to delay our 1:00 tee off times or make us late for the Swiss Chalet. Absent is the soul hunger for heart-felt and life engaging worship in which we both sense the presence of the Lord, are humbled by His presence, and challenged to give ourselves to Him for His mission.

If we will join God where He is working today, we may need to make some major adjustments of heart and mind. I was listening today to an African pastor talking about how Muslim people will hear the Gospel, but they often believe when they see the power of the Gospel. How long would you have to wait to see the power of God show up in our churches today in Canada?

Jeremiah's challenge to seek the peace and prosperity of the city to which the exiles had been carried requiring a real shifting of attitude and perspective, if they were to understand their relationship to God, their captors, and God's calling on their lives. They needed to see God first, not the things to which they had attached Him. When they were released from their bondage to "things" they would be able to see that God was not homeless in the ruins of the Temple in Jerusalem, but He was very much present with them in Babylon.

God's missionary call to Judah was first a call back to Himself, to a right relationship with Him from which doing right things would flow, not the reverse. It was secondly a call away from the distraction of "things". If you are travelling on a long journey, it makes sense to try to pack lightly since you have to carry what you take. God was calling Judah to hold lightly their attachments that they might be able to discern the difference between the things that last and the ones that do not. Sometimes the lines get fuzzy for us when we confuse our will with God's. Thirdly, Judah's missionary call was to the Babylonians. This was a hard pill to swallow, but it clearly was God's mission, and His intention was that it would be His redemption performed among the Babylonians through the Judean exiles. Judah, however, had to recognize that they were living on the harvest field, that those fields were ripe, and that they were the intended instruments of God for gathering it in. A hundred other missions might have been more palatable to the exiles, but this was the one they got. Like it or not they were God's agents for the redemption of Babylon.

The attitude of the exiles could not have held more emotion than it did. These Babylonians were barbarians in their eyes, a people not to be associated with. Yet consider for a moment what might have happened had Judah refused the word from Jeremiah. The result would have been only a deepening of the resentment, anger, and hostility towards the Babylonians. Sadly, the voices of the false prophets catered to this, and as a result the captors were seen as the enemy, not as a lost people they could help.

We also know from Israel's history that this people had a pretty good track record of complaining. If they refused to heed the word given through Jeremiah it is entirely possible that they would simply have fallen into the rhythm of complaining with serious consequences. If they grumbled and complained about their lot they would really have been complaining against God, who was trying to get their attention, not the Babylonians. "Seek the peace and prosperity of the city to which I have carried you!" It was God who had carried them off, not Nebuchadnezzar and it was God who apparently wanted to bless the Babylonians through them. Lurking underneath all of these layers was a message to Judah, that God wanted to have an ongoing love relationship with them not one of duty, and if they would join Him, they could find the place of His presence once again. It was also a immense revelation that He wanted the same kind of relationship to the Babylonians. Now that was shocking! The exiles may have been able to justify their grumbling and complaining in their own eyes, but they would do it before God to their detriment. If the truth were known, most of us can justify anything if we want to badly enough, and Judah had developed some skill at it. As one who pastored for over forty years I've seen a lot of people justify behaviors that left me scratching my head.

The modern corollary is shocking when we examine the attitudes of church people to their community. Many see the city as the enemy to be forsaken whenever possible, either by moving to the further reaches of suburbia, or by leaving for cottages each weekend. The violence and crime we equate with portions of our cities cause us to insulate ourselves in "gated" communities even though crime shows up there as well. Many see people of other religions in the city like Muslims, Hindus, Mormons, etc. as the enemy as well, and in so classifying them reduce the responsibility to reach them.

Unfortunately, these perceptions probably have more to do with fear and ignorance, our lack of an apologetic for our faith, and their polished responses to us. As long as the perpetrators of violence and crime are unknown to us we seem be able to sit passively while each day lost people head towards the Great Abyss without Christ.

Not unlike the exiles we complain about our cities, about bureaucracy, pollution, crime, immigrants taking away jobs, about having to be sensitive to people of other ethnic origins and religions, and about sin and evil around us. We don't seem to understand that we are neither in the majority as Christians nor are we part of the powers weaving the national fabric. We do not seem to grasp the depths of our estrangement within our culture when we think we can legislate the changes we want. As noted earlier, missions are finding greater receptivity to the gospel in the Muslim world in states which have sought to enforce strict Islamic law and religion. People have responded to oppressive demands by looking elsewhere such as to Christians in a spiritual rebound effect.

Craig VanGelder writes about the shifting away from 1.) the assumption of the Church being a part of the establishment in Canada with its privileges and of 2.) being the moral voice for the nation. [4.] Those days are historical reading for the Church today. The establishment looks to legislate answers while missionaries look to influence society one person, one family at a time. Jeremiah called the exiles and I think calls the Church today to an attitudinal adjustment. He was calling them and us to right action. Seeking the peace (shalom) of the city was seeking its welfare. The word "city" here probably refers to all the cities of Babylon to which the exiles were dispersed, and their call was to bless the city not curse it, to care for the city not abandon it. The exiles were to care for the city as if it were their own. This was radical. The people of God were to actually be initiators of peace and blessing, instigators of positive action, and involved in getting their hands dirty to clean up the sewage literally and spiritually of their cities. Tragically too many congregations today seem to be more than a few straws short of a broom when it comes to seeking the good of all people in our cities. Our style is to leave the running of and caring for our cities to the politicians, though we rarely bless them in what they do. The day may come, and God forbid it should be so, that we may get the politicians we deserve. So many people live in our cities, so few take responsibility for them.

Seeking the shalom of the city means promoting its wholeness by our efforts. It is impossible in urban ministry today to not be involved in youth and children's ministry in one form or another. Yet congregations inevitably have to deal with things like the wear and tear on the building, behavior unlike the saints (though not as different as many maintain), and the time and money spent on people who don't come to our fellowships. Sooner or later, it seems, some saint will stand up come budget time and ask why we spend so much money, time, and energy on this group which contributes little, and sadly often the youth ministry is made redundant. Even more tragic is when the non-churched kids begin to attend and the parents of the churched kids say, "I don't want my kids hanging around with 'those' kids," and they then both pull their kids and the resources from either the youth ministry or the congregation.

What hope do the unrighteous have if the righteous keep running away and hiding? Gangs may fight in the community with guns and knives while church people fight with words about worship, management, reaching "respectable" people, and servicing the saints. Strangely, in the Church today we seem to expect new Christians to arrive at worship fully developed in their sanctification and maturity, and don't want to have to be involved in the messes that often precede and follow faith in Christ. When you ask people how they came to Christ very few will tell you that they did so as a result of an altar call in a worship service. Most will say they responded because of a relationship, a friendship, a community that did something which caught their attention and led them ultimately to the Saviour. The old saying is true for today, "people need to know we care before they care what we know." It's reminder again of the incarnational nature of ministry in the missionary context of our cities and our world.

Many of the veteran saints in our congregations have had enough faith to survive depressions, recessions, two world wars. a host of other wars, floods, earthquakes, etc., yet they express fear and doubt about the future of our faith communities. If Christians can recover the missional nature of the Church, our communities can be much different places. I believe that the Church as the winsome Bride of Christ may have its brightest days to shine ahead of her. Seeking the peace and prosperity of the city will be part of that and comes into a different light in the lamp of Proverbs:

11:10 *"When the righteous prosper, the city rejoices."*
11:11 *"Through the blessings of the upright the city is exalted.*
14:34 *"Righteousness exalts a nation, but sin is a disgrace to any people.*

When the righteous begin to be the actors on the community stage, caring for the elderly, the shut-in, teaching those the school system says are unteachable, feeding the hungry, helping the homeless make new starts rather than just giving temporary shelters and handouts, raising the standard of life by the standard of self-sacrifice, and changing lives through so many other credible expressions of the love of Christ, then we will be truly seeking the peace and prosperity of our cities.

When I was a kid growing up in Sydney, I remember our church being a centre for friendships, for helping each other, for bettering the community, having fun and discovering Christ. In particular, I remember Men's Club Christmas parties, where the kids all got presents, where at one such party I got a brand-new hockey stick worth its weight in gold to me. I also remember great family events like the combination workdays at the camp and church picnic with all the games, ice cream, and soda pop you could imagine. I also remember at one of those picnics an elderly saint guiding my hand on the saw and with the hammer as I made my first frame. To this day I don't know how to frame but the moment was priceless to me. These were times of young and old together, the young refreshing the old and the old mentoring the young, times where relationships were formed, friendships forged, and where the values of the community were re-reinforced.

Somewhere, much of that changed, and its influence in the community changed with it. Somehow, the saints need to rediscover how to live in Babylon, how to laugh and have fun together, how to bring the young and the old together to refresh and mentor each other, how to serve together, how to live inclusively in our communities of faith rather than exclusively, and how to live and love like Jesus.

In our Sunday evening services we would once a month turn the worship service over to the youth and their pastor seeking to bring all generations together. On one of those nights our youth director led a study on "blessing" and then in small groups with a mixture of ages, with parents and children in the same groups they were to answer the same questions. Towards the end he had the adults form three groups and the youth one, to write blessings for the other age group. It was more than interesting to hear the blessings the older group gave the youth and see their response. It was also interesting to watch the adults as they were blessed by the youth. One of the things I observed is that blessing encourages blessing.

What if congregations across our communities discovered the power of blessing their city? What if we discovered the joy of being together, serving together, and building our community together, not just as local congregations but as groups of local congregations? What if our congregations hosted block parties to celebrate our communities? Would not some of the stereotypes about "Church" be broken for those outside the gates? What if the captives became the life-givers to their captors? Is this not the mission Christ has called us to fulfil?

ENDNOTES

1. Douglas Alan Walrath - Leading Churches Through Change, PGs. 36-37

2. Henry Blackaby and Claude V. King - Experiencing God, Pgs. 232-246

3. Leonard Sweet - Soul Tsunami, pg.432

4. Craig VanGelder - The Missional Church, edited by Darrel Guder, PGs 46-76

CHAPTER 7:

PRAYING FOR YOUR CITY

Jeremiah 29:7b
"Pray to the Lord for it,
because if it prospers you too will prosper."

In January 1995 over 50 Toronto area pastors climbed aboard a bus and travelled two and a half hours north of the city to the Muskoka Baptist Conference grounds to hold a prayer summit. It was sponsored by the prayer committee of Mission Ontario with Billy Graham. Rarely if ever had so many pastors from such a wide variety of church backgrounds come together to pray for the better part of four days. Denominations and congregational leaders were present who had preached against each other, and the theological spectrum was as broad as the lake where we were. I think it safe to say that very few of us knew either what a prayer summit was, or why we were there, except that we knew we were supposed to be there.

What followed was four life changing days of prayer and worship with many divine appointments clearly taking place. Pastors confessed longstanding struggles with sin, discouragement, depression, while others sought guidance, who then received prayer. There was prayer for each other, prayer for our families, and always ending at the communion table at night which had been the operating table throughout the day.

On the first night Joe Aldrich, who was the co-leader of the event with Bill Moore, asked a series of questions: "How many people here are Baptist? How many are Pentecostal? How many are Nazarene?" and on he went through a list of denominations until he stopped at the last question: "Who cares?" Amidst the chuckles was a poignant moment. As we sat there in the circle, the denomination we represented really didn't matter. The Church of Jesus was and is bigger than our little titles and ministries. Over those four days brothers in Christ were reconciled from different denominational tags who walked across the floor to embrace each other and ask for each other's forgiveness.

In the years leading up to that event and the years following I have observed a change happening in the Church, especially in the city. Local congregations are finally realizing that the Body of Christ is bigger than either their denomination or their congregation. Christians are beginning to realize that our cities need to be redeemed and that we cannot do it alone; we need each other in the city. Pastors also are discovering that they need each other in prayer and accountability.

I spoke at a seminary chapel to students challenging them to find people they trust, with whom they can pray and be accountable because of the dangers, temptations, and pitfalls involved in ministry today, as local congregations struggle with institutional responses to real problems rather than with grace and honest seeking after the heart of God. As congregations are challenged to change and adapt to the new day in which we minister many pull out their swords and lance the irritant pastor or at least remind him or her of his place. As congregations face decline, they will seek all manner of managerial style changes, growth formulas, and new ministerial fads but they will not produce the desired results if the community of faith does not embody the grace and love of Jesus in both speech, attitude, and action.

One of the positive things that is happening is that people and churches are coming together to pray for their cities. Videos like "Transformations" and "the Harvest" [1.] produced in the 90's challenged congregations to work together and pray for their cities, and changes are happening. Concerts of Prayer, Colleges of Prayer, Prayer Mountains, and Prayer Retreats are becoming more common, and people are displaying greater commitment to the Church at large. A few years ago when a new Free Methodist congregation was being planted in the Malvern area of Scarborough the local Baptist congregation in that area not only blessed the work but got behind it and supported it financially and otherwise. At one point in Scarborough we been getting the congregations along the Warden Avenue corridor north of the 401 Freeway to come together on the last Sunday evening of each month to pray for our city. We also looked at producing an evangelistic flyer to be used by the congregations bordering a new housing development in our neighborhood which would provide one flyer with all the churches listed rather than competing flyers. Something is happening today which in years gone by would not have taken place in our congregations so easily.

Something was also happening in Babylon. The exiles in a complete re-orientation of life and thought were being called to see their oppressors as an opportunity and their captors as their mission field. They were being called to change their attitudes and actions. Instead of calling down curses they were to pronounce blessings. Perhaps nowhere else was the challenge to see things from God's perspective more pronounced than in the call to prayer. Their submission to God would be seen in their prayer lives and how they prayed for the Babylonians.

For about twelve years I was been privileged to be a part of a prayer group which included pastors from Baptist, Christian and Missionary Alliance, Apostolic, an Associated Gospel Church, and me, a Presbyterian. On any given Sunday we pray for blessing in each other's congregations in our services as well as for the surrounding congregations. When I moved to Ottawa I went into withdrawal without that group and so I started asking local pastors if they would join me in praying for each other and our churches. There is now a consistent group of leaders in Orleans who pray for each other our churches, and our city each week.

Why do we do that? Because we know that as each congregation is "blessed" it raises the spiritual water level of our city. The more people are in church getting right with Christ the fewer the problems we will have in the city. I remember hearing Edwin Orr speak about the Welsh revival when such a wonderful movement of God took place that all that was left for the local constabulary to do was to arrange quartets to go around to the various churches and sing in their services. I long for the day when my city may be as wonderfully changed by the grace of God, and I believe prayer is the key to seeing it happen.

"Pray to the Lord for it.....", said Jeremiah. "The harvest is plentiful, but the laborers are few. Ask the Lord of the harvest, therefore, to send out workers into his harvest fields," said Jesus to

the 72 as he sent them out to the villages and towns to which they would go and preach. Prayer is primary on the journey whether it is in preaching the gospel, blessings homes, or healing the sick. Every part of these instructions from Jesus involves some dimension of prayer.

At one point in our ministry in Orleans God put a burden on our hearts for the community of Rockland, fifteen minutes east of us along the Ottawa River where new homes were being built at breakneck speed to meet the housing needs of the area. Before we did anything by way of ministry, we started prayer walking the community until every street had been covered. We went with two prayers, one for the blessing of the community, the businesses, the schools, and families, and the second asking the Lord what His will for us was in Rockland. By the time we had prayed through the community it was clear we were being called to begin a work there. A miracle or to later and we had space to begin our ministry. As we continued to pray God opened the way for a youth drop in and before long, we had on average of fifty young teenagers, mostly unchurched with all the noise, hormones, and chaos that they could bring and that we could handle coming and hearing the Gospel each Friday evening.

It has long interested me that when Jesus spoke to the seven churches in the Book of Revelation, he addressed them as "the Church in Ephesus", "the Church in Smyrna", etc.

It would seem from the perspective of the Lord that there is one Church in the city not a collection of churches or denominations.

This might further be amplified when we remember that in the early Church it was largely comprised of house churches with elders in every city but not necessarily every house. There were also occasions when the house churches would come together collectively in the city. As Jack Dennison points out, the majority of epistles in the New Testament were written to such churches. When Paul appointed elders, he put leaders in place who would exercise responsibility for the Church in the city. [2.]

This is a bit of a shift in understanding from where many of us in the Church today are. The time has come to recognize we can no longer afford to work for our own little fiefdoms, but that we are accountable to and for all the Church in our community. When the congregation around the corner is struggling it affects the whole Body. When the pastor is struggling, and many are today, the whole church suffers.

A number of years ago a congregation in our city went through an awful implosion resulting in the removal of the pastor. The congregation was not of my denomination, but it was one for which our congregation had some affection due to things we had done together and the relationship between the two staffs. It was also a congregation that had been a leader in the prayer movement in our city. There was not a lot of apparent outside help coming from the denomination they were in, so during all that took place another pastor and I attempted to facilitate some healing among the staff members of that congregation. In many ways I had no right to do so since I was neither in their fellowship nor their association, but it hurt to see a sister congregation being destroyed from within and the pain in the lives of friends not being addressed.

I would love to say that a wonderful reconciliation took place, but I am afraid it was only partial, and the congregation ultimately faded into the ether. Why would we try to effect healing? Partly because of the friendships involved but more so because what happened there affected the Church in the city. This was a congregation which had been the leader in our city of the prayer movement and in many other ways. When one congregation struggles it affects the Body.

Over the years in ministry, I have met with numerous pastors who have been hurting, broken, and discouraged, some from my denomination, most not. I do so not because I have a messiah complex thinking I have solutions to everyone's problems, but because I know that the Church needs good pastors with good hearts, and minds for the things of God, and if I can do anything to keep pastors and their churches healthy and moving forward, then I cannot afford to shirk that responsibility. The Church in Toronto, of which Scarborough is a part, was bigger than my congregation. The church in Ottawa, where I now live, is bigger than the congregation I served.

For the exiles to pray for their captors, the internal walls had to come down. They needed to see the bigger picture of what God was doing and what He wanted them to do. In II Chronicles 7, at the dedication of Solomon's Temple, God speaks about the responsibility of the people of God for their own national and local welfare. When the blessing of God is removed from the land and it became unfruitful, when the blessing of God on the people of the land was withdrawn and their health suffered, where does God say He look first?

> vs.14 *"If my people who are called by my name,*
> *will humble themselves and pray*
> *and seek my face*
> *and turn from their wicked ways,*
> *then will I hear from heaven*
> *and will forgive their sin*
> *and will HEAL THEIR LAND."*

God is saying there is a correlation between the faithfulness of His people and the prosperity of the land. "Seek the peace and prosperity of the city....and pray for it." To do that we need to clearly understand both the place of cities in what God is doing today and where they fit in the Bible.

We recognized earlier that God is urbanizing the world and internationalizing our cities. The nations are gathering in the urban centres of the world, and on our doorstep and cities once mega are now multi-mega. A city like New York has the equivalent of half the population of Canada within its boundaries. I remember taking my Dad to a Blue Jays game many years ago and as we sat there in the crowd of 50,000 I said to him, "Look around you! Right here you probably have the population of Cape Breton Island where we grew up."

Historically, there were substantial cities already in existence in the ancient world like Ninevah (7th century BC) with a population of 120,000. In the major ancient empires were major cities; Babylonia in Babylon, Ninevah in Assyria, and Jerusalem in Israel.[3.]

As Ray Bakke reminds us, the Mediterranean became the focus of the urban world in the later Greek and Roman Empires, with Rome in particular having a population of around 1,000,000 people. Rome continued as the major urban centre for the better part of fourteen centuries until the focus shifted to Northern Europe due to Atlantic trade.

The Industrial Revolution in the 18th century shifted the locus to Europe, Britain, and North America, and as major centres developed along these routes, by the latter part of the 20th century the major cities of the Pacific Rim began to be more prominent players.

Biblically, cities are featured prominently in both the Old and New Testaments. Hebrew and Greek words for "city" occur about 1200 times referring to almost 120 cities. Some of the prominent cities in the Bible are:

Sodom: This city became so corrupt and bankrupt of mercy that it was rejected by God because of its evil. It is also the city for which Abraham interceded, but which apparently was considered a disposable community by the godly as ten righteous people could not be found in the whole city. (Genesis 18-19)

Ninevah: This city had just over 27,000 people known as the Nazis of the Middle East and who captured the northern tribes of

Israel. It was the city confronted about its sin by Jonah which then underwent revival. It is a city whose story tells of God's love for a nation outside of Judah and Israel, extended through an unrepentant racist, who himself had to be converted to see that God's love goes beyond national boundaries. (II Kings 17-19, Jonah.)

Babylonia: This was a conquering city which itself got conquered from within. The captivity of the people of Judah led to the conversion of the King and the nation as Daniel and his band successfully integrated their faith into a foreign culture. It is the story of the conversion of the captives (Judah) as they discovered that any place is holy when God is there. It is the story of integrity under fire by Daniel and his friends, and it is the story of the conversion of a nation by its captives. (Jeremiah 29, Daniel 1-6)

Jerusalem: This was a city with a long history, conquered and crowned by David. It was the Royal City of David and the seat of power in Judah. It was the city over which Jesus wept and where he was betrayed and crucified. It was the starting place of a Pentecostal Fire which has burned for 2000 years. It is symbolic of the Celestial City of God.

As you read the Scriptures you see cities of various descriptions either related to their function or character, even personality. Jerusalem was the Royal City where the King lived. (Psalm 48, 24:7) Solomon built storage cities (II Chronicles 8:4,6). Rehoboam built safe cities with walls for defense. (II Chronicles 11:5-12) and there were intercessory cities which were sometimes also cites of refuge. (Numbers 35) The city has always been a significant part of the movements of God's Spirit. Follow the missionary journeys of Paul and you get a travelogue of the major cities of his day.

One might ask why cities of refuge to which murderers could flee would also be intercessory cities? The presence of the Levites might suggest that intercession and atonement for sin might have been part of the reason.

It is hard, when thinking about the potential of cities like Montreal, Toronto, and Vancouver, Halifax, essentially cities of refuge in in Canada where people from all over the world find refuge, to not also see them as centres of intercession for the nations. The potential is there for these great cities of the world to be life-changing cities as centres for intercession and salvation. The potential is also real for our cities to be given names after their personalities like Babylon the Great, Mother of all Prostitutes and Abomination of the earth. (Revelation 17:5)

What are the implications for our cities? When Joshua and Israel stepped across the Jordan to enter the promised land they did so based on God's command. The entire nation of people was charged with possessing the land as a united force. The previous inhabitants had so "ripened" in their sin that they were 'vomited" (Leviticus 18:25) out of the land by God. Israel would many times due to its unfaithfulness also find itself thrown out of the land.

Implication # 1: The Meek Shall Inherit the Earth.

Ministry today needs to focus on following God to the inheritance He has for us. As we pray for our cities it is healthier for us to see the people around us as needy rather than the enemy to be conquered. If there is conquering to be done let it be our souls by the love and mercy of Jesus and those around us by the tangible expressions of the same. To that end we need to start working for the little victories of grace won in the trenches which lead to the big victory and stop looking for the big one that will totally transform our cities while we do nothing. We need the little victories like the one broken person at a time healed, one family preserved at a time, one community centre at a time established, and one neighborhood at a time changed.

I noticed a pattern among church people years ago when we would bring churches together to pray for the city. They would be fired up with enthusiasm in the first meetings but when major revival didn't break out next month their passions cooled substantially.

Praying for our cities does not preclude asking God to do one big miracle, but it is a recognition that the Church has a big hill to climb. Praying for our cities works best when we follow God's commands in obedience, doing the things He calls us to do. The meek shall inherit the earth not because they are trying to take cities away from people but because they are trying to give them back better ones. It's that incarnational model again. As we stand with people in their struggles, we gain credibility for the gospel we proclaim. The people in your workplace who may seem most unresponsive to the Gospel may actually be the first ones at your cubicle when a wheel falls off of their lives and they are struggling. Then we have the opportunity to put our arms around them and say,

"When I was going through something similar is how my faith in Christ sustained me."

The way in which the tribes possessed the land is informative for the Church in the city. Joshua rallied the tribes to take the different cities of the promised land one at a time though only one tribe would inherit any particular area. They all fought together (Numbers 32, Joshua 1) for the greater victory not as individual tribes but as a nation. Is it conceivable God is gathering the nations into our cities for a great harvest? If so, then it is time to pull together.

Implication # 2: Cities Need To Be Seen As Neither Neutral Entities Nor As Disposable Environments:

Praying for our cities begins with praying for people; friends, neighbors, family members, and work-mates who may have different values and lifestyles than we do. Cities and people often embody the values they espouse, and these days the chances are pretty good that those values won't change by argumentation since they were not likely arrived at through a process that was as logical as it is emotional.

Those values may change however, when something happens in a person's life that exposes their weakness, and we are there to show the love of Christ. As we pray for people, we must be prepared for those "kairos" moments, when life's twists arrive unannounced for someone, where we get the corresponding tap on the on shoulder from God and hear His whisper, "Now! Go, help, and share how I helped you in your weakness."

We also need to challenge the mentality which seeks refuge in the further reaches of suburbia rather than staking a claim in the determining of the nature of a neighborhood. What happens when there are no longer ten righteous in the neighborhood? What fills the vacuum created by the departure of the saints? God muddied His hands in creating us and bloodied them in redeeming us.

Can we do less for those around us without Christ? To do so may just lead to city transformation. Our neighborhoods are no more disposable than the people who live in them. Less of a we/they attitude may mean we stop objectifying people to our and their detriment. In our urban communities we need to acknowledge our fear that Muslim and Hindu neighbors may have been better schooled in their apologetic than we are, but also realize they are real people who struggle with many of the same issues we do. Like us, they struggle with the secularization of our children in the schools, and with teen-agers who are not owning for themselves the family faith. At the same time we need to do something about our apologetic weaknesses and grace deficiencies in loving our neighbors.

I recently heard of a couple thinking about leaving their neighborhood because they are weary of chickens not only being kept in backyards but also of the head-chopping which accompanies it for the religious festivals of their neighbors. I couldn't help but remember the stories my mother told of the chicken exploits in her home in Louisbourg and recall that it was not that long ago that we ushered our own chickens from the barnyard to the table. Life today has become so sanitized that unless our chicken comes from KFC, Mary Brown's, or Swiss Chalet it is considered uncivilized.

Praying for the city means praying for the neighbors who keep chickens, or drink too much, or party too late at night. I see one of my neighbors going out for her walks on a regular basis who prays for our neighborhood as she goes. I wish more people did. In so doing you meet your neighbors, known and unknown, and can quickly develop a list of people and things for which you can pray. If you want to meet your neighbors get a dog. You will soon have all kinds of conversations with people in your neighborhood. They won't all be spiritual conversations, but they plant seeds. It is even possible to solicit prayer requests on these occasions. Strangely enough, people who know you are praying for them, appreciate it whether they admit to believing in God or not. It is a form of caring that is meaningful, and one prayer at a time, one answer at a time, one relationship at a time a neighborhood can change.

Implication # 3: The Enemy Is Not the Church Next Door-

We have seen the enemy. It is not us. God calls us to possess the land together (Joshua 1) and to rebuild the broken walls of the city together (Nehemiah 4:13-23). As we labor for our cities we do so as brothers and sisters in Christ together. When the trumpet sounds we gather at its location to shore up the defenses. Our fight is for our neighbors, our families, and the children, but our partnership is not based on familial ties, ethnicity, economics, nor denominational bonds but on Jesus Christ, the Great Shepherd, who searches for the lost lambs. We do well to remember what it was like when we were the lost lambs, often not knowing we were lost, so that we can reach out with tenderness to those around us. Jesus wept over Jerusalem. Who weeps for your city?

There seem to be barriers keeping us from taking seriously the Great Commission in our cities, even though many of the people who come here from around the world get converted and then go back to their places of origin with the gospel. Bakke lists a number of things which have kept us from being effective such as:

1. *Church politics that either prohibit or preclude involvement.*
2. *Superintending bodies like Presbyteries or Synods.*
3. *Egos that have to be massaged.*
4. *Budgets and other bureaucratic snares.*
5. *Not enough organized prayer.*
6. *Too few properly trained leaders.*
7. *The failure to seize opportunities for witnessing.*
8. *Ghettoized Christian living.*
9. *Non-cooperative congregations.*
10. *Busy saints with too many church meetings.*[4.]

To this list we could add things like the loss of nerve in proclaiming the gospel in a pluralistic culture which trivializes truth, resistance to real change, and the naive hope that if we huddle together in our fellowship and hold on to each other long enough either the final cataclysm will come and we'll be safely escorted "home" or revival will come and we still won't have to do anything. Luke 12:35-36a

Kenon Callahan wrote in 1990,

"The day of the churched culture is over, the day of the mission field has come..... The day of the local church is over the day of the mission outpost has come." [5.] If the day of the mission outpost has

come then our seminaries and Bible Colleges in the West need to reorient themselves to producing missionaries rather than pastors and academics.

The fire of revival has touched down in places around the world today, usually ignited by the united prayer of people and congregations desperate enough for change in their cities to overcome their fears of each other, to hold hands together in prayer, intercede for God's mercy, and then work to show it.

"And pray to the Lord for it (your city), because it prospers, you too will prosper."

God grant that the righteous may prosper in our cities and exalt our nation bringing transformation to individual lives, families, and our communities.

ENDNOTES:

1. Videos: "Transformations" produced by the Sentinel Group, 1999

        "The Harvest" produced by Integrated Resources Limited, 1997

2. Jack Dennison - City Reaching, Pgs. 44-48

3. Ray Bakke - The Urban Christian, Pgs. 28-29

4. Ray Bakke - The Urban Christian, Pgs, 45-60

5. Kenon Callahan - Effective Church Leadership, Pgs. 13,22

CHAPTER 8:

KNOWING YOUR SEASON

Jeremiah 29: 10-11
" This is what the Lord says:
'When the 70 years are completed for Babylon,
I will come to you to fulfill my gracious promise to bring you back to
this place.
For I know the plans I have for you,'
declares the Lord,
'plans to prosper you and not to harm you,
plans to give you hope and a future.'"

In a study done by a school in Iowa it was determined that the production of 100 bushels of corn from one acre of land required 4,000,000 lbs. of water, 6,800 lbs. of oxygen, 5,200 lbs. of carbon, 160 lbs. of nitrogen, 125 lbs. of potassium, 75 lbs. of yellow sulphur, other elements too numerous to mention, plus rain and sunshine at the right times. Although many hours of labor from a farmer are required it was estimated that only 5% of the produce from that one acre can be attributed to the efforts of man.

What is required to produce a harvest in our congregations and our cities these days? Judah was having to learn something about the different kinds of fruit produced in the soil of humanity and the different seasons involved. They found themselves in exile even after God had warned them to shape up before they were shipped out. They chose instead to encourage the message of the false prophets more suitable to their hearing. (Verses 8-9, cf. Chapters 1-2) As they slowly began to clue into God missionary purposes for them it would mean recognizing the seed they had sown, the seed they needed to sow, and the season in which they were living.

God through Jeremiah told the exiles to put down roots, to be productive influences, to be stabilizing factors, to seek the peace and welfare of the city, and to pray for it. He also told them to stop listening to the messages of the false prophets and to instead, listen to the truth from God. In the opening chapters we touched on the confusing voices today and their impact on the Church.

As we recognize the false voices and our culpability for our predicament, like the exiles, we begin to shift our focus from being victims to being responsible. God had shifted the focus of the exiles from their desires to the needs of the people around them, and in so doing, He addressed their greatest need for repentance and right action. The exilic reality was that for a season (70 years) they were going to be residents of Babylon. They could choke on the proposition or make the best of it.

When the Word of the Lord came through Jeremiah saying: *"When the 70 years are completed for Babylon, I will come to you...."* they were being reminded that something bigger was going on. Though it was Judah in exile, the completion of 70 years somehow related to Babylon. In other words, it was a season for Babylon, after which the Lord would fulfil His promise to Judah.

The exiles were being reminded that God's thoughts were not for their destruction, nor the destruction of Babylon, but for their instrumentality in each other's lives to find the heart of God and come into a love relationship with Him. God assured them that they would neither be forgotten nor forsaken, and that if they plugged their ears to the false prophets, heeding the Word of the Lord, then they would become His agricultural instruments in the Babylonian harvest fields.

As such the measurement for Judah would be God's thoughts and plans not their imaginings. (Verse 11)

> *"For I know the plans I have for you (I know the thoughts I think about you), plans to prosper you not to harm you, plans to give you hope and a future."*

Their gauge would be truth not words that sounded good and warm. Their hope would be in God's plans not theirs. Their strength would be the assurance that God was in control and moving toward fulfilment of His plan, no matter how unpleasant it felt in the moment. Terry Wardle recently made the comment that it is often the things we think will break us that most form Christ in us. It's a reminder that God is always at work, that He never sleeps, that he is always working His plan. (Romans 8:28-30) For Judah all of this was to recognize the season of the Lord in their lives and the lives of their captors.

The Season of Preparation: Judah at this time may well have felt that nothing mattered because things always turned out so badly. They may have even felt that God's will stunk and that He was the Eternal Killjoy, having thrown them in among the Babylonian barbarians. Nevertheless, if anything good was going to happen correction had to take place and they would need to recognize both God's hand and His timing in their lives. They might have to get to the place Joseph was when he said, "What you intended for evil, God intended for good." Judah needed to understand that God's season for them was a season of preparation.

When a farmer gets ready for planting, he prepares the soil by loosening it, harrowing the soil, breaking it up, removing the stones each spring raises from below so that the ground is receptive to the seed. He does not sow the seed on hardpack because it brings minimal results, but he does tend to the field until it is ready. The soil which is broken up may have laid dormant for some time producing nothing, or it may be a well-used field, either of which may require a dose of fertilizer or compost to make it ready for the seed.

> God had spoken to Judah in Jeremiah 4:3-4:
> *"This is what the Lord says to the men of Judah and to Jerusalem:*
> *"Break up your unplowed ground and do not sow among the thorns.*
> *Circumcise yourselves to the Lord, circumcise your hearts...."'*

The warning was to get the fields of their lives in order before the cultivator came through and forced the issue. He was saying prepare your lives through repentance, break up the unplowed ground of your hearts or I will do it for you. They were called to a season of soil preparation.

> *Psalm 51:17 "The sacrifices of God are a broken spirit, a broken and contrite heart O god, you will not despise."*

Judah needed to break up the unplowed ground of their lives; attitudes of superiority which were not productive to the plan of God and speculations which didn't fit God's future for them. Fruitless lives full of smugness towards others and God, lifestyles that were barren, and ponds of self-pity to swim in as they sang their victim laments, would all have to be changed. There may have been much built in Judean lives but apparently it was mostly weeds and of little Kingdom value. Jeremiah's call to break up the unplowed ground was a call to again live productive lives in line with the will of God. Their season of preparation/repentance was about shaking loose all the things that didn't matter in the light of Eternity, all the things from the periphery of their lives which had become central, all the habits of speech and behavior that were not only unproductive, but unbecoming of Kingdom bound people, and all the false influences, bad inputs, which allowed the weeds of sin to grow.

I don't think it's much of a revelation to say that there is ground in the Church today that needs to be broken up. Like Judah, there are many attitudes, many defense mechanisms, many false voices to which we have listened, and many sins hidden which must be shaken loose for us to be productive soil for the seed of the Lord. Not unlike Judah there is a need for us to rediscover the primary missional nature of the Church, to reprioritize ministry around kingdom values not sentimentality, to refine our standards of morality, to re-fire holy passions, and reject what is both unproductive and destructive. The Lord was saying: "Here is a window in time and opportunity (kairos) I am opening for you. Will you be prepared to do something in it." Jeremiah 19:11 records another warning:

> *"This is what the Lord says: 'I will smash this nation and this city just as the potter's jar is smashed and cannot be repaired.... vs. 15 .... because they were stiff-necked and would not listen to my words.'"*

In case we haven't grasped it yet, we need to understand how important it is to listen and respond with obedience when God speaks. Otherwise, if we refuse, our circumstances may turn against us, and the ground may break up underneath us, until we are finally prepared to listen. As God had prepared the soil of the exile's lives so also had He prepared the lives of the Babylonians for this time.

Judah had a calling from God to be missional in their understanding of themselves and their relationship to Babylon.

What is God saying to the Church today, especially in the cities about the soil of our ministries? What is He saying to us as individual Christians about the soil of our lives? Are there elements of our lives and ministries God would like to shake loose so we may take hold of Him and His purposes for us? Maybe God is asking us to see our neighborhoods and communities through His eyes!

The message of God comes with the purpose of affecting change. We can either be changed by it or judged by it. Whatever the season we are in may be, we can be certain about one thing; that God wants to draw us deeper into a love relationship with Him that stirs our affections for the world around us. Blackaby puts it well when he writes: "He (God) wants you to experience an intimate love relationship with Him that is real and personal." [1.] and "His (God's) desire is for you to become involved in what He is doing."[2.]   A number of years ago after I had announced I believed God was calling me into ministry my mother gave me the following poem from an unknown author.

If His hand in wisdom closes
Every avenue there is
To the service you would render,
Don't forget the work is His.
Do not fret and lose your patience
If He bids you sit and wait.
In His own kind loving manner
He will open another gate.
If He shuts you up in silence
At the folding of the hands

It may be that in His furnace
He is burning off your bands.
And when all your gold is molten
In His crucible of flame
He will lead you into service
That will glorify His name.

II. The Planting Season:

I read about the 100th anniversary celebration of Christian missionaries going to a particular area of Zaire. A full day of long speeches had taken place culminating with an old man coming before the crowd insisting that he be permitted to speak. He said that he would soon die and that he had some important information which if not shared would go with him to his grave.

He explained that when Christian missionaries had come 100 years earlier his people thought them strange and their message unusual, so the tribal leaders decided to test them. The test consisted of slowly poisoning the missionaries to death. Over a period of months and years missionaries and their children died one by one.

The old man said: "It was as we watched how they died that we decided that we wanted to live as Christians." Those who died mysterious deaths never knew why they were dying or what impact, if any, their lives and deaths would make. They stayed because they trusted Christ and loved those they served.

If the cities in Babylon were in a season of preparation, then logically the next season for them would be the planting season. As Judah would learn to trust that God had brought them to this place for this time, they would be able to plant the seed which would ultimately lead to a harvest. If the season of preparation is about getting the soil ready, then the planting season is about seed selection and planting it where it would grow.

As the season of preparation gets lives ready to sow the seed of the gospel, the planting season refers to the witness of our lives individually and as a community of faith and the kind of seed our lives sow.

Jesus said in John 12:24

"Unless a kernel of wheat falls to the ground and dies,
it remains only a single seed.
But if it dies it produces many seeds."

The exiles could stay in their holy huddles of self-pity and self-preservation waiting for their trial to end, essentially hosting pity parties for themselves, and crying the victim, in which case their trial might go on indefinitely. They could insulate themselves against the vile Babylonians and preserve the seed for more "worthy" recipients, and therefore forfeit the crop, or they could instead, as a scattered people scatter the influence of their lives in Babylon. They could in the words of Hosea 10:12:

"Sow for yourselves righteousness, reap the fruit of unfailing love and break up your unplowed ground. For it is time to seek the Lord until He comes and showers righteousness on you."

God has been wonderfully bringing to Canada today people who have come from places which we would only have dreamed of meeting in years gone by. Even more so, the ease of travel has facilitated people travelling to and living in places we only read about previously. Not only are people living in strange places but in many cases being paid to work there. The ease of working remotely today has opened up untold possibilities of how to define "remote." I have a friend who splits his time between Thailand and the US who works as a business consultant who inevitable when he is on one side of the globe or the other is coaching/consulting through the internet.

Not long ago a Tamil family living near our Church invited my family to share with them a meal and a prayer meeting in their home. There we sat with a family who had lost everything including family members in the war in Sri Lanka, who in their humble circumstances lavished us with their generosity. It was both wonderful and terribly convicting at the same time as I compared the comfort and ease of my life to theirs.

At the same time, considering my upbringing in the east coast of Canada, then finding myself in a Tamil home in Toronto, thrilling at the opportunity for a relationship with this family reminded me of the fantasy I live each day in such a cosmopolitan city, rubbing elbows, and sharing a meal with people from around the world.

Our world has changed, and our cities have changed with the world. Unfortunately, our churches have not always embraced the opportunity these changes have brought. Our churches need to change to once again, become the mission outposts of vibrant, winsome Christianity such as was in evidence in the first century, where the seed can be broadcast and a harvest of changed lives gathered in.

When you are one of the scattered called to sow it is important to sow the right seed. We don't need any more seeds of bitterness in our fellowships or between them to be sown. We don't need the hybrid seeds of self-pity, anger, strife, slander, division, self-preservation, or traditionalism. We have raised too many crops of those weeds in the past and as a result have rendered the Church irrelevant to the eyes of the watching world, which is hungry for spiritual truth and a sense of the meaning of life found only when the soul rests in the Saviour. We sense the thirst for something more from those around us saying in its own way: "Sing for us the Lord's song!" (Psalm 137:1-3)

Our present planting season requires the pure seed of the love of Christ which reconciles and heals; the seed of truth given with grace, the seed of righteousness expressed in quality living not holier than thou attitudes, the seed of faith evident in trusting God to provide for our needs as we give of the resources God has provided for us for the benefit of others, and the seed of joy which illustrates the new life within. No more Christians baptized in vinegar and weaned on lemons need apply. What we need are real Christ followers with a real faith in the real Saviour living in the real world. It is time to plant the kind of Christian seed which can blossom and bless those touched by it, the kind of seed that when it blooms releases the fragrance of Jesus Christ to all within a nose of us.

It is time to glorify the Lord and enjoy Him, beginning now and lasting forever. We have seen and experienced the "Christians" who have had the ability to smile and speak with honey dipped words which carve out the liver of any person who was different view or didn't submit to our agenda. That we don't need. We do need Christians who

> *"Stay alert. This is hazardous work I'm assigning you.*
> *You're going to be like sheep running through a wolf pack,*
> *so don't call attention to yourselves.*
> *Be as shrewd as a snake, inoffensive as a dove."*
> *(Matthew 10:16 The Message)*

Today we are reaping a harvest of closed churches and consumer Christians, perhaps the fruit of our "religious" seed, instead of the fruit of changed lives from the missionary seed we should be sowing. It is time to put the right seed in the soil but that requires of us a right recognition of the soil conditions we are dealing with.

Carey Nieuwhof in a recent blog noted seven church trends that will disrupt 2024:

1. The stable church has become an endangered species. Studies show that the church today is either growing or declining with not much in the middle.

2. Millennials are now the new core of your church. They are embracing church attendance faster than any other demographic.

3. Gen Z will start to reshape the church. It is expected that the next era of the church will be "less produced, more personal, less performance based, more authentic, and finally, less head driven, more heart driven."

4. Discipleship has a growing digital component. Digital

Discipleship tools have been mostly a neglected tool until COVID sent everyone home to the internet. It is anticipated that churches that will make a difference will be more digitally present.

5. Partisan extremism will continue to fuel short-term church growth(but not long-term growth. Though hardline stances in the cultural and political wars can result tin short-term growth, over the long haul they tend to simply poison the water of the evangelical church. The church needs to be prophetically courageous but prudent about whether it is a Gospel stance.

6. AI (Artificial Intelligence) will become normative in growing churches. "almost everyone has embraced AI widely and rapidly, except in the church, where it's been greeted mostly by yawns, disinterest, and leaders' pontification on how it should be condemned. Right now, only 19% of church leaders say they use AI on a daily or weekly basis.

   That's about to change quickly.

   As 2024 opens, many start-ups and entrepreneurs are creating new software to help churches leverage AI, and legacy companies and brands are integrating AI into their existing software.

7. A new kind of megachurch pastor will continue to emerge. Many of the leaders replacing megachurch pastors embrace a very different style of leadership style that will be:

- "Less top-down and more consensus-based.

- Less interested in popularity and platform and more interested in local ministry.
- Less concerned about their name getting out there and more concerned about leading well in their context.
- Less focused on bringing back the past, and more focused on building a new future.
- Less fixated on size and more fixated on health. Ironically, with that focus, many are now leading a church larger than that of their predecessor. [3.]

Judah had not only had the seed of their lives prepared, but God had been working ahead of them in Babylon preparing the soil there for the seed to be sown. The exiles needed to know and see the readiness of the soil and respond accordingly, just as we do. The captors asked the captives for "songs of joy, the songs of Zion" suggesting that the soil conditions were ready for a planting of the seed. Like the exiles we need to then plant the best possible seed that will lead to a harvest of righteousness in people's lives.

The soil of our culture has been described by many today as Post-modern indicating that it is after the "Modern Era" and therefore different from the age of enlightenment, rationalism, and human potential which marked that age. Instead, the Post-modern world is one of cynicism, the relativity of all truth, individualism to the extreme, loss of corporate consensus as to the values on which we base our lives and communities.

While "Post-modern" is an adequate term for our day it creates a certain mindset which has its identity in what is over. The reality is that we live in an unchurched, pagan culture, a pre-Christian world. I choose those words intentionally because they speak, not of something that is over but something that is about to begin. In the post-modern smorgasbord Tolerance is the god du jour. Claims of truth are branded as narrow-minded, fundamentalist, phobic and a whole host of other caricatures. Truth is no longer something cognitively known but personally experienced. Logic is out, argument from the extremes and exceptions is in. Individualism determines your course; "If it works for you, it's true." and what you do believe does not have to be logically consistent, as very few actually bother to examine whether their personal philosophy or religious track actually makes any sense.

Many people function in life with philosophies of life handed to them by television commercials intended to sell a product, but which have in reality sold the soul of the nation for a profit. Truth is where you find it, yet we never consider our inconsistency when we go to the doctor.

If I have a tumor growing out of my forehead, I am no longer content to say it is all relative, or have a doctor tell us that it is whatever we want it to be. We want truth. We don't see the inconsistency of our lives related to truth when we are not content to have the teller at the bank say that all our money is the bank's since it is all relative anyway and be refused access to our funds, but we are prepared to dismiss Gospel truths as relative. We live in a logic free, no-fault world driven by individualism supreme and with personal preferences the ultimate value, to the point that our culture now tells us we can choose our own identity regardless of how God made us.

The church responds to our times with a mixture of shock and despair and carries on in its missional paralysis. We live not in a Post-modern world but a Pre-Christian one, which in terms of the Church's response should be a very different headspace.

We can't sit back mourning what was, grieving our fall from dominance but instead we seek from a position of vulnerability, one by one to change the world with the love of Jesus poured into our hearts and lives for others to taste.

We should also recognize that the soil of our world is international. As we have noted God has been bringing the nations into our cities. To put the right seed into the soil we need to be not only familiar with our own beliefs but also be prepared to enter into conversation in the marketplace of ideas as to why we follow Jesus. As our cities become increasingly international and the world undergoes changes of its own, we also see an increase of tribalism, the conscious and determined loyalty to whatever our group or tribe is, be it ethnic, ideological or religious..

We've seen in recent years in politics and social agendas where if you have any slight difference from what I think, you are the enemy to be shouted down as we then retreat to our particular tribes for reassurance of our polarized beliefs. As personal distinctives get lost in the shuffle of the global community and the pressures of culture, the gravitational pull for identity through heritage becomes an almost irresistible force.

When all other values are thrown off ethnicity becomes the last undeniable personal value and therefore to be guarded, even defended at all costs. The movements toward independence in eastern Europe and even Quebec are expressions of that search for identity. In Quebec the Roman Catholic Church for decades as the dominant power framed all sense of identity religiously but in the absence of religious values Quebecers now find their identity in rallying to the linguistic and secular flag.

Strangely, it seems that the more people search for identity more it results in isolation, emptiness, and alienation. Not knowing who we are in Christ means we look elsewhere for value and significance, essentially in the valuation of self and de-valuation of others who are different. One of the bad seeds the Church sowed for decades was this kind of self-valuation pitted against those not as "biblical", not as "charismatic", not as "evangelical" as we were. In this headspace those who differ are the enemy even if it is only in minutiae. As a result, now people turn to family, work, cultural groupings, the local pub to provide the values which put our guilty souls at ease.

Present in the midst of this context is a search for "spirituality" in non-traditional forms, traditional forms having rendered themselves irrelevant either by heavy-handed tactics, confused and contradictory voices, or embattled isolationism. There is an openness but not to archaic expressions of Christianity or religious presentations.

Many seek quick fixes and instant cures for their ills and character flaws leading many to various forms of meditation or "spiritual" practice. The religion most desired, it seems, is the one that makes few moral and character demands. To be appealing the spirituality proffered must seem non-religious which actually works in favor of the true Christ follower who in seizing one of the greatest opportunities ever presented to the Church is then able to talk not about religion but about a relationship with God through Jesus Christ.

On its way to estrangement the Church has had generally one of two responses to the changes occurring. The first has been accommodation, choosing largely to follow the agenda or standards of the surrounding culture thereby becoming a "spiritual" veneer hiding the deeper flaws.

Unfortunately, it confuses the identity of the Church in so doing, because it becomes too difficult to tell who is driving the bus, God or culture. If the Church has the same message as the culture only veiled in spiritual language, who then needs the church? Why would anyone want the religious garb of churches indistinguishable from culture?

The second response, typically by conservatives and evangelicals, has been isolation with hostility. Today, it seems like conspiracy theories abound about government and the world we live in. Churches retreat with guns blazing at anything remotely different, with little love, and lots of judgement. As a result, on the way to the fringes evangelical churches lose credibility through their absence from the field. Neither response has allowed the Church to be the revolutionary voice of a counterculture bringing correction and inspiration to the narcissistic trance in which society finds itself.

A third response though not often exercised, is to neither adopt culture nor retreat from it but to be a counterculture within it, fully engaged with our world yet grounded in the truth of who we are in Christ and who God is as revealed in His Word. It means we are not prepared to endorse everything of our society as being good or even value-neutral because it says so, especially without legitimate reason.

The Bible with all of its relevance has to frame our responses to what is happening around us. When culture is out of step with truth, we seek with grace to restore truth. When the world in which we live in perceives that we care enough to come down out of our ivory towers to get our hands dirty in the clean-up and recovery of our neighborhoods and cities maybe then credibility for the gospel will be restored. Maybe then it won't be so easy to dismiss the church as irrelevant.

The season for today's missionaries and for the church today is a planting season, planting the kinds of seeds which will grow the right crops, healthy ones. The spreading influence of the gospel through credible sowers ultimately should result in better citizens and therefore better cities and nations. Clearly that is a goal to which no one could object. In that light we should recognize as followers of Jesus then that it is also the season to die to self (John 12:24) and to die for the Babylonians.

I Corinthians 9:22.

"To the weak I became weak
to win the weak.
I have become all things to all people
so that by all possible means I might save some.
I do this for the sake of the gospel
that I might share in its blessings."

It is time to re-enter the world with the gospel of Jesus Christ, not to win people to our side or ideology but to bring them to the person of Jesus where real life can prosper and flourish.

The Harvest Season: It is amazing to see the mission strategy of Jeremiah 29 put into practice in the life of Daniel and the changes that resulted. Who would ever imagine that exiles could so influence not only their cities but a country to the point that it changed, you could even say it was converted, but that is what happened. Time and time again when revival fires have burned communities where transformed.

The harvest season is but a moment in time. After preparing the soil, planting the seed, nurturing it and watching it grow, the farmer watches it grow and awaits that telltale sign that the season is right to gather the harvest. In that very moment every resource available is applied to bring in the crop before it spoils.

The exiles of Judah would plant a seed harvested during Nebuchadnezzar's reign, by Daniel and his companions. What tools will be used to today to bring in the harvest when it comes? Let me offer the possibility of at least three tools we can deploy today:

1. Authentic lives: As people today search for meaning and purpose Christians can live authentic lives, reflecting a real relationship to Jesus Christ with real love for our neighbors, (Mark 12:29-31) lives which are winsome and qualitatively different from those around us, lives prepared to answer with grace and truth when asked for the reason why we are different. Authentic lives also own that they are broken but under the Master Craftsmen's care they are being rebuilt often from the ground up. Our discipleship with Jesus so often involves as much unlearning of the world's values and ways of doing things as it does learning God's. That education rarely flows in straight lines in our lives but rather with upheaval, many twists and turns for which we did not ask.

Vulnerability then, a subject on which Brene Brown has done an incredible service for God's people desiring to be authentic, becomes more of the norm rather than the hiddenness that has characterized so much of life in the church.

In an age when the final authority is whether what we believe works, we need to be able to tell how following Jesus works for us, how having Him as our Saviour makes a qualitative difference in our lives. We can tell what it is to have been blind and now able to see, what it was to have been hungry and now be satisfied, what it is to be broken and healing under the Great Physician's care. The day in which we live places ultimate value on personal story. It is time to tell ours with grace and compassion and in so doing tell of the Good Shepherd and His love for lost sheep.

2. Authentic Community: Anybody can tell the difference between an authentic body of believers and a collection of religious people. There is a life, a vitality, a qualitative difference in the relationships, in the way they speak to and about one another, and in their way of looking at the world. An authentic body of Christ followers is not a museum for religious relics but a hospital for hurting and broken people in need of attention from the Great Physician. At one time or another we all need a hospital whether it is to be born, or for surgery to correct something gone wrong, or to visit someone else who is a patient, or to provide or learn how to provide health care, or even to die. The Church could also be seen as a recycling plant for the renewal of both old faith and tread-worn saints, a classroom for pupils hungry to learn at the feet of the Master and generating station for Spirit-empowered ministry. Authentic communities of faith recognize that rarely are two people at the same place at the same time in their journey. They give grace to people, encouraging and inspiring them to grow, so that when they are "healed" they learn to be healing influences where God has placed them. The world is waiting to see if in this millennium the Church an authentic community of hope, healing, and truth will be.

3. Authentic power: Somewhere along the way the transmission fell out of the engine of many churches. They can still rev the engine, but there is no movement. Somewhere along the way to the periphery of life prayer became either forgotten, neglected, or dismissed and the Holy Spirit not only became a stranger but an unwelcome intruder due to either bad stories or bad experiences.

While the world watches we cannot attempt to do ministry with smoke and mirrors. It is with Jesus, in His power or it is nothing. It is beyond me as to how any Christian, let alone any

Christian community, can function with these two keys missing yet, it seems many do. We replace the Holy Spirit with programs and procedures as we pat ourselves on the back at our apparent cleverness.

As the fledgling Church of the book of Acts took its first baby steps, we see the Holy Spirit breaking in on believers regularly, challenging, empowering, guiding them until they got on the same page with the Father. In Acts 2, Pentecost is one of those Holy Spirit break-ins, as is Acts 8 seen in the outbreak of revival among the Samaritans under Philip's ministry, as is Acts 10 where Peter's racism gets challenged and cross-cultural ministry considered and Acts 13 where the Holy Spirit interrupts a prayer meeting to set apart Paul and Barnabas for intentional cross-cultural mission work, and on many other occasions thereafter. Today if the Holy Spirit doesn't vote with the democratic majority rule we are seriously confused and don't know whether to trust what we've heard.

There is, however, a dynamic, authentic, holy power needing to be rediscovered by Christians and the Church in Canada, if we will entertain any hope of seeing the harvest gathered. As Jim Cymbala once said "We can't do this ministry with smoke and mirrors. It's Jesus or bust!'

> *"In everything by prayer and petition,*
> *with thanksgiving*
> *present your requests to God."*
> *(Philippians 4:6)*

Prayer is not an option for Christians in a missionary encounter with their culture; it is an absolute necessity. It not only is able to settle disputes and calm ruffled feathers when together we seek the heart of God, but it also keeps us in touch with what God is doing and what he is inviting us to join Him in doing. Prayer keeps us focused on the Master Plan with the right responses of submission and obedience. It allows us to see when secondary things are becoming primary and peripheral things central. It reminds us that we need God's grace to accomplish anything and anything done without His presence is not worth doing. Praying together helps us see the blind spots and the gifts we cannot see in ourselves. Praying together helps confirm and fuel the vision of what Jesus is inviting us to do.

Similarly, we need the Holy Spirit to break into our ministries once again in Biblical proportion and fashion if we will be effective in our harvest field. Otherwise, all our plans, programs, dreams, and visions are but the revving of the engine. It may sound like there's lots of power but if there is no movement it is only a facade.

We need the Holy Spirit to re-orient our lives, ministries, and churches to Jesus, to empower us for His ministry not ours, to enable discernment of what He is doing and where He is going so we may join Him rather than constantly trying to get Him to join us. Authentic power is something only God can give but we are invited to ask, to make ourselves available, to be ready for Him and in so doing pray that we have not so grieved the Holy Spirit as to extinguish the fire.

For the Church estranged in Canada and beyond there is hope. It lies not in ourselves nor our devices but in repentance and faith that positions ourselves before Jesus for His moving us to where He is working. It is about our recognizing His hand on our lives, our cities, our nation, and then being prepared to let Him plant us as His seed and be gathered into His harvest.

Today it is time for pastors, people, and churches to put down roots, be productive influences, be stabilizing factors, seek the peace and prosperity of our cities, to pray for them, and be prepared to act at the command of the Lord in the season of the Lord. The farmer may only be responsible for 5% of what it takes bring in a harvest, but he/she is still required.

A one-legged schoolteacher once presented himself to Hudson Taylor, the founder of the China Inland Mission (now Overseas Missionary Fellowship), volunteering for service in China. Hudson Taylor surveyed the teacher and asked this question. "Why do you, with only one leg, think of going as a missionary?"

George Scott replied, "I don't see those with two going, so I must!" He was accepted.

The Church in Canada stands on one leg, shifted to the periphery within its own culture. It cannot wait for someone else to change our predicament. We too, must go to the lost and lonely, the poor and the wretched, to the alien and the orphan, the violent and the drug addicted, to the rich and the homeless of our neighborhoods, our cities, and our nation. We have the Lord's song to sing in the land of our exile, a land whose inhabitants are saying in a hundred different ways, "Sing us the Lord's song, Sing us the songs of Zion!"

O Canada, our home and native land.
True patriot love in all Thy sons command.
With glowing hearts we see Thee rise,
The true north strong and free.
From far and wide O Canada, we stand on guard for Thee.
God keep our land glorious and free
O Canada we stand on guard for Thee
O Canada we stand on guard for Thee.

Lord of the Lands beneath Thy bending skies,
On field and flood where e'er our banner flies
Thy people lift their hearts to Thee
Their grateful voices raise -
May our dominion ever be a temple to Thy praise.
Thy will alone let all enthrone
Lord of the Lands make Canada Thine own,
Lord of the Lands make Canada Thine own.

ENDNOTES:

1. Henry Blackaby and Claude V. King: Experiencing God pg.1

2. Ibid.   pg.29

3. Carey Nieuwhof   https://careynieuwhof.com/church-trends-2024/

CHAPTER 9:
COMMUNICATING THE GOOD NEWS

Jeremiah 29:12-13
"The you will call on me and come and pray to me, and I will listen.
You will seek me and find me
when you seek me with all your heart."

Cousin Angus had been out playing hockey with his buddies at the local arena and their ice time having expired they were all back in the dressing room recovering, rehearsing their exploits from the game, and getting changed when the cell phone next Angus started ringing. After a few rings he picked up the phone, put it on speaker, and answered it.

Hello" said Angus.

Women on the other end: "Honey it's me. Are you at the rink?"

Angus: "Yes."

Woman: "I'm at the mall now and found this beautiful leather coat. It's only $1000.00. Is it OK if I buy it?"

Angus: "Sure, go ahead if you like it that much."

Woman: "I also stopped at the Mercedes dealership and saw the new models. I saw one I really liked.

Angus: "How much?"

Woman: "$60,000.00"

Angus: "OK, but for that price I want the winter tires and the sport package."

Woman: "Great! Oh, and umm … one more thing… the house we wanted last year is back on the market. "They're asking $950,000.00."

Angus: "Well, go ahead and make them an offer, but not over $910,000.00"

Woman: "OK, see you soon. I love you!"

Angus: Bye, Love you too." And he hangs up.

The guys in the room who had heard all of this are looking at Angus with sheer astonishment until he looks up and says:

"Anybody know whose phone this is?"

Well, the good news for Angus was that he wasn't going to get the bills from the phone call. What's the good news for us though, as we navigate our place in this world as followers of Jesus Christ and as part of His gathered community?

Can I suggest three aspects of the Good News for us in the context of Jeremiah 29 and the lessons the exiles were being invited to learn.

1. God Has A Plan: Jeremiah 29:10-11

"This is what the Lord says: "When seventy years are completed for Babylon, I will come to you and fulfill my good promise to bring you back to this place. [11] For I know the plans I have for you," declares the Lord, "plans to prosper you and not to harm you, plans to give you hope and a future."

After Judah got the bad news from Jeremiah that they needed to unpack their suitcases, settle in, put down roots and become productive, stabilizing influences seeking the peace and prosperity of the city to which God had brought them, he then gives them the good news. That being, that despite how harsh they may have felt their circumstances were in that moment, God was at work in and through them and He had promised that when this moment had passed there would be a good result.

The old saying is that it is always darkest before the dawn. The problem is it is still dark before dawn and at times that darkness can feel overwhelming, like dawn may never come. In many ways that is the way it feels in Canada today. This week the government determined that our military chaplains involved in Remembrance Day services would not be permitted to make any reference to deity in their prayers or comments, a ruling that should go against the convictions and conscience of any person of faith, which supposedly are enshrined in our constitution. We see moral agendas being driven in both public and separate school boards which tolerate no exceptions or contrary beliefs. A young man living northwest of Ottawa has been suspended from school for the better part of the last year because he dared to say that there are only two sexes, male and female and he is being charged in the courts related to his beliefs. The darkness does indeed seem to be deepening but that is not all of the story.

The good news is that, just like in the day of the Judean exiles, God is still at work, still redeeming people, still transforming lives and making them more whole, still breathing life into valleys of dry bones. I am reminded from church history that there have been many times when the darkness deepened, and God's presence changed individuals and communities.

To go back to the story of Shrek, God's people have been the catalysts for the restoration of more than one swamp, as they have been driven on the winds of the Holy Spirit.

In the midst of a world that seems to be spinning into chaos, where there are more refugees and displaced people than at any other time in history, where the intoxication of power drives political and social agendas, there is also a greater openness to hear a message of hope and life. We've known for years that when people move within

Canada, for the next year they are more receptive to new ideas because of the changes they have experienced. How much more is that true for refugees and displaced people coming from heavy handed governments who caused their uprooting? We've seen in Africa Inland Mission how the more heavy handed the government is the more people, especially the younger generation, turn away from the religion and values of their governments. We've seen that people coming from creative access nations where sharing the Gospel is illegal, willing to listen to the Gospel and commit their lives to Christ.

Let's not kid ourselves, the life of the exiles was not easy. No one will give you a free pass because you have some faith convictions any more than they did for Hananiah, Mishael, and Azaraiah when they were thrown into the fiery furnace, or when they, along with Daniel defied the dietary and religious laws of Babylon. But they still became people of influence within the nation.

The good news is that God still has a plan, that he is still working it, and He still invites us to be light and salt in the midst of darkness, giving us what we need to be faithful in the moment. He still invites us to be a part of seeing lives transformed for the better, brought into greater wholeness, and given meaning and purpose. It does require some adjustments on our part however, to join God in what he is doing, and it begins with loving our neighbors and loving our communities. One of the reasons why we started the new church in Rockland was because every time I drove through the community my heart grieved for the people of the town and the absence of life-giving churches there and so we began to pray about what we should do as we prayed for the town. We have the opportunity today to be life giving people where God has planted us but that takes us to the second part of the good news.

2. God Hears Our Prayers:

Jeremiah 29:12

> *"Then you will call on me*
> *and come and pray to me,*
> *and I will listen to you."*

God through Jeremiah reminds the exiles that they are not in Babylon by themselves and left to their own devices, but that God is also with them and attentive to prayer. We are reminded that wherever God is, is holy ground, a place of encounter and commissioning. Does He always give the answers we want? No! Often the answer God gives involves some change in us.

Think again about God's answer to Solomon's prayer at the dedication of the Temple in II Chronicles 7:14:

> *"..if my people, who are called by my name, will humble themselves and pray and seek my face and turn from their wicked ways, then I will hear from heaven, and I will forgive their sin and will heal their land."*

Contrary to the belief of many today, the healing of the land does not begin with unbelievers getting their act together, it begins with the people of the Lord getting right with God. He calls us to humble ourselves; our attitudes, our opinions, our judgements of others, our hearts before Him. What does God look for but a humble and contrite heart. (Isaiah 66:2) He looks for people who seek Him, not people who seek something from Him.

So many of us treat God like a holy vending machine. If I put in the right payment (works, service, performance) God is bound to give me what I want, but that is not remotely close to who He is. God doesn't need to be convinced to love us or bless us. He already does. He has *"plans to prosper you and not to harm you."* He is always working His plan which includes what is best for us, no matter how painful in the moment, and His plan always involves the greater/bigger picture of what He is doing in the world. Going back to Henry Blackaby's reminder, God wants an intimate, ongoing, dynamic relationship with US. That's what drove the incarnation of Christ and ultimately His death and resurrection. God wants us to be in relationship with Him.

Peter in writing to a group of people scattered because of the persecution that broke out in Jerusalem said this to them in I Peter 4:16-17

> *"However, if you suffer as a Christian, do not be ashamed, but praise God that you bear that name. [17] For it is time for judgment to begin with God's household; and if it begins with us, what will the outcome be for those who do not obey the gospel of God?"*

So one aspect of the good news is that God has a plan but the other part is God is invested in us and how we can be better reflections of His name, character, and Gospel. That investment grows and is clarified in our surrender in prayer. What did it take for the exiles to be willing to submit to God? It took a good dose of humbling circumstances. Isn't it interesting that it often takes the same for us to finally get on our knees before the Lord?

Therein lies good news for us. When we finally get to that place of desperation God meets us in prayer and is waiting for us to seek His face not for what we can get but for whom He is, to stop living as our own masters and submit to the loving One.

The good news for the church today is that God still hears and answers prayer and if anything is ever going to change in our nation it will begin with God's people on their knees. I used to have a sign on my office door in the last church I pastored that said, "The Church can rise no higher than the height of her leaders on their knees." Changing our world begins with changing us and that happens in prayer. But here is one last aspect of good news for today that is worth remembering.

3. God IS Present:

Jeremiah 29:13-14
"You will seek me and find me when you seek me with all your heart. ¹⁴ I will be found by you," declares the Lord, "and will bring you back from captivity I will gather you from all the nations and places where I have banished you," declares the Lord, "and will bring you back to the place from which I carried you into exile."

For so many of us when life takes a twist we didn't plan or want we assume God has left the building, but nothing could be further from the truth. It is usually in the darkest, murkiest, most challenging events of life that we find God doing His best work in our lives. I've learned that the places in my life that represent the deepest pain can be transformed into places of sweet embrace when I meet Jesus in them. Such is the power of His presence. I have seen on so many occasions that when something I didn't plan for or see coming around the corner arrived that God had already been there putting in place the things and people, I would need to keep my nose above the water line.

When the Judean exiles landed in Babylon, they discovered that God had been there ahead of them preparing the soil and that He was now interested in preparing them for the mission field they were living in. God's presence changes things.

When we were pastoring in Bobcaygeon, Ontario I experienced something I had never seen before. We had a group of ladies who every Wednesday morning met for Bible study and prayer which I discovered was the power behind all we did in ministry. I lost track of the number of people who would come up to me after a Sunday morning service saying, "As soon as I walked in the building, I could so sense the presence of the Lord that I couldn't stop weeping throughout the service." For a short time, I thought my great preaching had something to do with it, but I quickly disposed of that thought realizing that the real power was in that prayer group and that because of their prayers the veil between heaven and earth grew very thin when we gathered in worship. God's presence will do that.

No matter how dark the moment may feel before dawn we do well to remember that God is still present. One of my favorite verses in recent years has been from Exodus 20:21:

*"The people remained at a distance, while Moses approached **the thick darkness where God was.**"* (Emphasis mine)

It reminds me that in whatever darkness I may find myself God is present there. I can testify that in the darkest moments of my life the Lord has met me in profound ways and brought breath to my flickering soul such that not only would I not exchange them for anything but I would say the darkness was worth it. So, if God can meet an old sinner like me in my darkest moments, He can meet you and He can meet His Bride, the Church and bring life. I don't know of anything more encouraging when you are going through a difficult time than knowing that someone is walking with you, that you are not alone.

The exiles were assured that they were not alone, that God was present, that he was working His plan, He was available in prayer to help them become the missionaries He intended them to be, and He would be with them through it all until they returned home.

We are living in a day when the effective church will not be the religious franchise on the corner but the mission outpost taking various forms in our communities as we seek to be faithful to the Lord who call us to the Great Commandment and the Great Commission. Jesus said new wine required new wineskins and the Church today needs both; the new wine that the Holy Spirit brings and the new wineskins (new ways and understandings about how to do ministry today) to hold it so it can be shared.

Ministry today is a logging road blazing a path for others to follow so they can get to the ultimate destination. The question for us is what part we will have in the effort to build the road so others can find their way home to Jesus. God continues to work His plan. He hears our prayers and He is present with us on the pilgrimage from the ruins to the Celestial City. He invites us to join Him in rebuilding ancient ruins and restoring places *(people?)* long devastated; in renewing ruined cities that have been devastated for generations, to be called the priests of the Lord and ministers of our God. (Isaiah 61:4-6)

It's an awesome task but it is and incredible honour to join God in His mission. Can we get out of survival mode and begin once again to be light and salt changing our communities one life at a time, one family at a time?

May the Lord who loves us so much that He sent His best, His one and only Son, so that whoever believes in Him may have eternal life, help us to give our best for Him and for the world for which He died, rose again, and to which He now sends us.

Today might feel dark but the dawn is coming and by faith in Jesus Christ we believe we can contribute to the light.

May we pray together the prayer of Habakkuk from Habakkuk 3:1-2

"A prayer of Habakkuk the prophet. On shigionoth

²Lord, I have heard of your fame;
I stand in awe of your deeds, Lord.
Repeat them in our day,
in our time make them known;
in wrath remember mercy.

Life is a Pilgrimage
(Reflections on "Life is a Journey from "Soul Friendship" by Ray Simpson)

The Christian Life is a Pilgrimage ...
From pretending to being real;
From a false identity to true identity in Christ;
From ignorance of myself to full disclosure;
From being scattered to being integrated;
From meandering through life
to life lived with purpose;
From a missing compass
to following the TRUE North & His compass;
From being broken hearted to living full hearted;
From disappointment to hope;
From insecurity to being safe and secured.
From fear to confidence.
From being ego-driven to Other centred;
From compulsion to Spirit controlled;
From grieving to healing;
From being the Captain of my own ship to
being a deck hand on the Master's;
From resignation to relinquishment;
From clutching to offering.
From living in the shallows
to plumbing the depths of Jesus' love;
From twisted perspective to seeing by faith;
From being tone-deaf to God's music
to dancing my heart out;
From sold out to the world
to bought at great price;
From being restless inside
to a settled peace inside;
From being empty to overflowing;

From being an orphan to a child of God;
Most of all it is to be loved
by the Prodigal Father
always watching for us to come home,
by gracious Jesus who substituted
His life for ours,
and by the Holy Spirit
always alongside to gift and guide.
Thankyou Lord for the Pilgrimage with YOU!

Manufactured by Amazon.ca
Bolton, ON

37553460R00098